ADAM Man Convoluted but GOD

THOMAS L. HAMPTON II

Copyright © 2021 Thomas L. Hampton II

All rights reserved.

ISBN: 978-0-578-86904-9

MEDITATION

With my mouth, I asked God for life, He heard my thoughts.

What I have received, I do not recognize.

What did God hear me think for He has blessed me with

what I have believed. He must have misunderstood...

For this baby is not my child.

God you said when I pray, you would hear,

if you heard, why am I bound? Why has the slave woman

conceived me and pushed me from her womb?

The prayer of Ishmael...

Then God answered him and said,

"Finally, a man has searched deep within himself and

thought."

This that you have asked, I have been waiting to answer

but first, I too have a question. Why do you believe in two

women? Why does man perpetuate the belief of the existence

of **Two Wombs**? Why the belief in duality? You were in

utero; she is not your mother!

ADAM Man Convoluted but GOD

Then one said unto him, Behold, thy mother and thy brethren **stand without** *(not a part of* **thySELF***), desiring to speak with thee. But he answered and said unto him that told him,* **Who is my mother?** *and who are my brethren?*

"The greatest evil that can befall man is that he should come to think ill of himself."

<u>Johann Wolfgang von Goethe</u>

THIS PAGE INTENTIONALLY LEFT BLANK

CONTENTS

Preface

Introduction   1

1. Let There Be Light.................... 32
2. The Day of The LORD.................. 57
3. Let Us Make Man in Our Image........ 85
4. Cognitive Dissonance & Superstitious Ideology   105
5. Man does not have to Die to go to Heaven   132
6. The Detriment of Religious Dogma.... and Promulgation of Fear   151
7. Acquiescence of the Mind................ 160
8. Inertia and Mass (The Woman & Rest)   175
9. About The Author....................... 187

   Bibliography............................ 195

THIS PAGE INTENTIONALLY LEFT BLANK

ADAM Man Convoluted but GOD

PREFACE

Ye men of Galilee, why stand ye gazing up into heaven?" The furious preacher asserted that the doctrine taught by Galileo in Florence, of the earth's revolution round the sun, was quite irreconcilable with the Catholic religion, since it glaringly contradicted several statements in Holy Scripture, the literal meaning of which, as adopted by the fathers, was opposed to it. And, as he further asserted, **'that no one was permitted to interpret the Bible in any other sense than that adopted by the fathers.'**

They will involve themselves in sad contradictions, nay, even in heresies and blasphemy, if they always interpret the Bible in an absolutely literal sense. Thus, for instance, they must attribute to God hands, feet, and ears, human feelings such as anger, repentance, hatred, and make Him capable of forgetfulness and ignorance of the future.

"As therefore," continues Galileo,

the Holy Scriptures in many places not only admit but actually require a different explanation from what seems to be the literal one…[1]

---

[1] Galileo Galilei: And the Roman Curia (Classic Reprint), 66-67.

ADAM Man Convoluted but GOD

Ask yourself one of the most thought-provoking questions and then identify the interpretation of the Church Fathers, who's literal interpretations of spiritually discerned word is yet restricting the spiritual maturity of those desiring to

Be the Resurrection of Christ.

The correct response to this question will liberate you…

"Men of Galilee",

why do you stand looking up to find heaven?

The Son of Man has no place to lay His head…

His brother would not give Him a home;

Let him live on earth in you…

The Truth of Resurrection is Rising In Man!

DEDICATION

This book is dedicated to years of positive and negative reinforcements, opportunities, and presentations. Successes and setbacks, illusions and delusions, trials, disciplines, uncertainties, and utter confusion have done this one thing for Man, 'caused them to think'. By the sweat of your brow shall you eat your food, Adam… Thank you Father for the Earth has fed me well… The experience has caused them to Evolve… The sweat of your brow was only a Good Father saying to His children, "I'm going to force you To Think" …

Adam, You Are What You Can Become, and what you can become, already exists for you are what you can become… Adam is God Atomized.

Let me explain, what you can be is coming into the world of being because you are… Still don't understand? Read this scripture in the light of what you just read and think of it as the Eternal Image or picture of who was to come before the first man was made known, he was in the Mind of God as the Perfect Blueprint… **1** In the beginning was the Word, and the Word was with God, and the Word was God; **²** this one was in the beginning with God; **³** all things through

ADAM Man Convoluted but GOD

him did happen, and without him happened not even one thing that hath happened. ⁴ In him was life, and the life was the light of men, ⁵ and the light in the darkness did shine, and the darkness did not perceive it. Listen again, He was in the World, but the world did not perceive Him. Was He hiding somewhere out there in the ether? No, He was in man, but man hid Him and wanted to die to go to heaven where He was, but He was in the World of Man...

Now, whatever you can imagine about yourself, you can become because everything is possible and God did not limit you, man has. God created you with Infinite Potential, the pattern of your greatest self already exists in Spiritual Form, God is waiting on the body; The Physical Man to agree with the Spirit and He will Become You...

This book is about Man, Man with a capital 'M' because of who we are. The word Atomize means to reduce to <u>Atoms</u> and every atom is Christ for all things came through Him. If you can hear me, please say Amen... Atomize - to split into smaller parts, sections, groups, factions... So that He that existed before the particles were made known, He who is unseen may be known by what is seen... Adam is but the comprehensible substance of the

ADAM Man Convoluted but GOD

incomprehensible All. The whole could not be understood all at once, so God Created The Atom. Therefore, this Adam to whom this book is dedicated was an introduction to the world, One man, who in Him existed all. In other words, the simplicity from whence complexity arises… Adam Man Convoluted, but God…

Oh yeah, concerning God's creation, He gave it all to His Son…

And whatever the man called a living creature, that was its name. There was not a living creature alive that was not named by the Man. All that existed, God allowed His Son to **Name…** God called the Man Adam who was made in His Image giving him the authority to name creatures: anything living or existing. "When we think of creatures, we think of Animals, but Adam and Eve gave names to more than animals, They created the Environment of the Garden by what they saw in it!" Adam was given this authority after all was finished, finished meaning possessing infinite potential to become… God's work was finished on the 7th Day, everything created after that day was the work of the man and his wife: Imagination. All that was, everything that existed, Man named. To name is to have dominion over those things that exist. The reason unnatural creatures are alive in your

ADAM Man Convoluted but GOD

Garden Adam and Eve is because you saw them there, you have Imaged them there by the Power of Infinite Potential…

Yes, even that Serpent that you imagined in that tree. We name according to how we see… God provides the presentation by which we Ebb and Flow in and out of what is known as 'Mental States' of mind with which we create our environments. Thus, we elevate the physical and subject our spiritual superiority to the creature of imagination, unknowingly releasing spiritual dominance to those things which should not be, sickness, lack, poverty and even death because of temporary states of mind. Every unnatural creature is the result of the name given to an image of the mind. Man ultimately chooses to dwell in Earth, in Heaven or in Sheol… The creatures in your Garden Adam and Eve are the direct reflection of the Heaven or Hell where your soul is, even now, your soul is resting in its eternal home… Yes, you make Earth the exact replication of your spiritual home… As above so below, Jesus said, "These things I do, I saw my Father do in Heaven." Why do you see what you see in your Garden? Before Adam became (physical existence), He existed with God or was in God as His thought. Adam became the representative here on Earth of who was in "Heaven".

ADAM Man Convoluted but GOD

Genesis 2:7 reads literally: 'and he became the Adam for the life soul'. The particle that means 'for' is left out in translations so that our translations fit our theology. Quatum Phaith, by Jeffrey Strickland

God brought the Animals to Adam to see what he should call them; God caused Adam to Think. To think of himself differently than the other creatures or beasts. Man became man because he could apprehend God by thought. He was not arbitrarily naming animals; he was thinking about his relationship in the Kingdom of God. When Adam said there is no mate for him, he began to think as a Man not beast. This story is speaking of man's evolution of mind from Cave Dweller to Modern Man not simply a man looking for a mate. This book is dedicated to Adam because Adam and Eve sacrificed their lives in the garden so that we might live the life by learning their story as we live, we can read our lives as they have already been played out by Adam and Eve. The story of Adam and Eve is about more than an isolated Garden experience, but an evolution of the Mind and Life of Man. Man is Dust, the snake will eat Dust, Let us rethink this Matter of Dust…

ADAM Man Convoluted but GOD

THIS PAGE INTENTIONALLY LEFT BLANK

ADAM Man Convoluted but GOD

Introduction...

Physical Adam is a biological entity, sharing attributes with millions of plants and animals, he is a creature, an animal made alive by complex systems of intertwining eternal Life Substance. In him are Centers of Ganglia; Inner space imaging of Outer space, other worlds and interacting Galaxies. Man is, if you will, a Microcosm of the Universe, smaller in mass, larger in degree of purpose. In every man, there exists a Heaven known only to the man himself. Just as there are many galaxies, in man are many experiences, creations and inventions of which he is ruler and keeper because without him, He cannot be made known. Since this is the case, when what is in him is revealed, he is Lord and what he has made manifest is his kingdom. What he chooses to make known is only a superficial glimpse of his inner world.

A World, even a Kingdom is every Man known and represented superficially as Matter, even as the grey matter of the Brain lacks insulation, the outer man lacks insulation from the outer environment, becoming product of the environment made alive according to what he can Conceptualize. Therefore, coming to the realization; "that which is in him may not be known by what covers him." By what covers him, he has made his world known and uncovered it. Every Idea like a Star, its appearance deceiving the natural mind. A celestial body, spiritual by nature of representation; a light in the mind, a great mass of energy, producing worlds beyond carnal imagination.

An Effigy of Christ...

Appearing at first a distant spark, now Life sustaining Substance that Matter. Such are the Evolutions of Thought; thus, Man is His own Master. Who has made Him? From whom comes his authority? Let us look for Him in the sky, no man has yet seen Him. The world he creates, only He alone can live, many portraits have been drawn to scale Him but He alone paints. Any man who comes after him must live in an illusion for He is only one, His story has only been told.

The Vicariousness of Christ...

Too often we limit the fullness of our lives by attempting to live our lives through the experiences of a person who is believed to have lived a greater life than our own. By doing this, the only life that is ours to live is minimized and instead of focusing on being great in this present life, heaven becomes the afterlife. For your information, there is only one life that exists. God did not create two, but one life and man is to believe in that life and make it his own. Jesus came and walked the earth and lived an extraordinary life because he believed in but one life. Abraham came and lived his story and, in his life, found heaven on his journey to Canaan. Each man finds life when he is willing to take the journey to find that City. The Blessing was not in Canaan; the Blessing was in Abraham. Canaan was a manifestation of what Abraham believed while he was yet in transition represented by Chaldea. Terah, Abraham's father knew of God, but his God existed in the stars, far away from man. God in the likeness of the man's own imagination, shaped by the reality of that which evolves is the Omnipresent God; He was in Abraham. No man can find Abraham's God for none other is Abraham.

God is very present and not far away, the Evolution of the Mind.
Where the man is, God is there; He will be with Him,
His Image not known by another's experience of Him.
Let the man who knows God write his story by the life he lives.
Countless lives have vanished, and the light refused to shine,
the life He lived was not his own,
who he was, has not been known,
for it was not He who lived.
You have been given a name by which none other can answer.
That which is light to you,
has caused your brother to fall…

Theology or Philosophy…

Many who have come in the name of truth have not known that those who taught the truth did not know Him. Did you know that the authority for certain religious doctrines were validated by the leading Philosophers of the age and if the belief did not align with the ideology of the philosopher, the spiritual revelation was not accepted as truth? Did you know that who man is said to be, the substance of which he is made was first formulated in the minds of those who themselves were also made? Who you believe yourself to be may not be the self-unmade but the self that has been made by Man. Come out from Among Them… Be the Him, The Only Begotten Son who is not made and unmade by them.

Not many have recognized the correlation of Philosophy and religion.

"Philosophy is defined as the pursuit of wisdom, a search for a general understanding of values and reality by chiefly <u>speculative</u> rather than observational means."

In the matter of understanding values and reality, what could be more valuable to the pursuit of wisdom and knowledge than for one to embrace the study of the nature of God and religious belief; Theology." In fact, *"The history of Christian philosophy begins not with a Christian but with a Hellenized*

Jew, Philo of Alexandria, an elder contemporary of St. Paul"² To gain the understanding of Christian thought and logic, the starting point must be with a philosopher. Not just any philosopher but one who lived in St. Paul's day.

It is further stated by the Cambridge history of later Greek philosophy that, *"According to Posidonius the curriculum designed for school aged children as their general education, i.e., grammar, rhetoric, dialectic, geometry, arithmetic, music, and astronomy, though neither philosophy in themselves nor productive of moral virtue, are nevertheless an essential preparation. They have the status of a 'servant', just as earlier primary education prepares the mind for general education.*

Philo takes this idea one stage further: the studies of general education prepare the mind for philosophy which in turn prepares the mind for the yet higher wisdom of revealed theology." Pg. 140

To see this in application, let us reference one of the authors of the Greek Bible. Paul, according to the Bible, began as a Jew named Saul who excelled in education as a zealous Pharisee upholding Jewish law against all heresies, false

---

[2] A.H Armstrong, "Cambridge History of Later Greek and Early Medieval Philosophy; Ed. by A.H. Armstrong," in *Cambridge History of Later Greek and Early Medieval Philosophy; Ed. by A.H. Armstrong*, First (Cambridge: Cambridge University Press, 1967), pp. 137-137.

doctrines, religions, and even philosophies. In a turn of events which included the relinquishing of a name which linked him to a heritage he once was willing to murder for, Saul became Paul...

(*The Complexities of man... For I do not understand what I am doing, because I do not practice what I want to do, but I do what I hate.*) according to his Hellenistic or gentile identity and ministry to which he now upheld as an Apostle of the Christian faith. (*And if I do what I do not want to do, I agree with the law that it is good.*)

Paul found himself by direction of the Jerusalem Church facing superstitious beliefs, Greek philosophies from Aristotle to Alexander the Great who learned Egyptian "Myth" from libraries in Memphis Egypt or Ancient Alexandria after the invasion of Egypt by Alexander and the Greeks. This Alexander was the son of Phillip II of Macedon who captured the city of Crenides and named it after himself, which was traditional for the conquering ruler to do, the city thus becoming Philippi. Crenides became Philippi with the religious beliefs formed and propagated by philosophers like Pythagoras, Plato, and Aristotle. Proclus Lycaeus called the Successor was a Greek Neoplatonist philosopher who believed that all Greek theology derived from the secret doctrines of Pythagoreans and Orphics. Orphism being associated with literature ascribed to the mythical poet Orpheus, who descended into the Greek underworld and returned. Orphics also revered Persephone who annually descended into the Underworld for a season and then returned and Dionysus or Bacchus who also descended into the Underworld and returned.[3] There is no wonder the Greeks could relate to the Christian doctrine of salvation through death, baptism and resurrection. These religious beliefs and philosophical foundations are those with which Paul were familiar and fought against as Saul. (*The Complexities of Man*) Defending of his faith requiring familiarity with the Philippian's doctrinal beliefs, so that Paul would become all things to all men that he may reach a few.

    The Christ preached by Paul had to satisfy the historical background and belief systems of the Philippians if Christ was to be conceptualized by those who formed the church in Philippi. Let me explain this Christ; before I can explain the Philippian's Christ, I must direct attention to the Jewish/Greek name Joshua/Jesus. The idea of one man dying

---

[3] A.H Armstrong, "Cambridge History of Later Greek and Early Medieval Philosophy; Ed. by A.H. Armstrong," in *Cambridge History of Later Greek and Early Medieval Philosophy; Ed. by A.H. Armstrong*, First (Cambridge: Cambridge University Press, 1967), pp. 305-305.

for the salvation of another was foreign to Jewish belief, see Ezekiel 18. Speaking under Divine influence, Ezekiel declared the Word of God saying, "The person who sins is the one who will die." Jesus' own teachings confirmed this in his parable of the sheep and goats in Matthew 25. Although many people fail to realize his message of salvation here. What a person does and how he treats those here on earth speaks for one's spiritual condition and dwelling of the soul. Where his treasure is, his heart is also... Those who were represented by the sheep, did not do those good deeds to Christ but did them in Christ, in the name of Christ, they healed the sick and set the captives free!

By nature of Paul's message to the Philippians, he did not preach Joshua the Jew, he instead confronted the Philippians with a message about the Transcendental Spirit (Ruach) in Jesus, neither Hebrew nor Greek. I could go further into explaining this Christ, but I would like for you to think about why a message about Joshua the Jew would not have been received with the same Transforming Power as the message of Christ. Paul was a dynamic speaker, more than that, Paul was a spiritual being able to speak profoundly and poignantly to the core/innermost substance of the individual. Paul the man was learned in secular knowledge as well as religious. For him to be successful as a Minister, Paul had to first **"Bind the Strong Man"**, His duty was in essence to Plunder one's spiritual/religious convictions: *"But no one can enter a strong man's house and plunder his goods, unless he first **binds the strong man**. Then indeed he may plunder his house."* Plunder his house? The Serpent said to the woman, *"Did God really say, 'You can't eat from any tree in the garden'? "No! You will not die, the serpent said to the woman. In fact, God knows..."* The serpent confronted her mind with a Transforming theology, a sermon, an idea that pierced her intellectual and spiritual aspirations... Plundering her traditional thoughts, the serpent not only spoke to Eve, but it also ministered to her...

And now, back to Paul, who after having set up the church at an undisclosed time of which we do not have record of a letter or physical church except as mentioned as a place of prayer. This place of prayer was according to M. R. Vincent not a synagogue but only a proseucha or praying place, a slight structure which was *open to air without walls or roof.* This structure was outside the city gate near a stream, the stream used for ablutions or ceremonial washings (baptism).[4] These washings were more probably used as pagan worship than for the worship of God for there were very few Jews in Philippi.

---

[4] Marvin R. Vincent, "Word Studies in the New Testament," in *Word Studies in the New Testament*, vol. 3 (London: Nisbet, 1887), pp. 530-530.

However, the purpose for this letter according to Köstenberger, Kellum and Quarles had several possible purposes, both pastoral and personal. Philippians 4:2 shows us one of the issues facing Paul and Silas, the disagreement between Euodia and Syntyche. Paul urged them to come together in the Lord in harmony. The apparent threat to salvation appears to have been false teachings, not from other Jews as were Paul but from Hellenistic paganism and philosophical persuasion from learned Greeks. In other words, Paul was having difficulty persuading the people of Philippi to get away from their culture's religion but to fellowship or the practicing of self-control, conforming to the gospel.[5]

Transcendental Christ did more and extended far beyond a local group of believers, He bridged the void between Hellenistic culture and social conditions. Paul's idea of Christ brought with it not only power to transform but faith in a universal Creator (*according to traditional thought*). His message and the idea of brotherhood between man, made possible by the realization of the internal Christ of which they could relate,

---

[5] Köstenberger Andreas J., L. Scott Kellum, and Charles L. Quarles, "The Cradle, the Cross, and the Crown: an Introduction to the New Testament," in *The Cradle, the Cross, and the Crown: an Introduction to the New Testament*, 2nd (Nashville, TN: B & H Academic, 2016), pp. 645-646.

pared to ideas and theology of some already existing beliefs.[6] The internal Christ being the Elder Brother, the Soul of Man; none other than "Adam" before the world changed his attitude of himself. Paul made it plain to the Philippians that it was this Soul, alive and working in them in contrast to Apollos and other Greek <u>Mythological</u> gods. *(let us think about what we have been taught to think… Did Paul convert the Greeks or did the Greeks convert Saul the Jew?)* The Transcendental Christ existed long before Paul ever was… Before Abraham was, I AM…

This book is conceived from the mind of a man who makes a clear distinction between religious and Spiritual, superstition and Faith, having once himself believed that miracles are different from applying principle. After 47 years of living a life guided by religious beliefs, the meaning and distinction of liberty rather than freedom in the Garden was realized. Man's freedom before the introduction of religion was better defined as Liberty independent of the knowledge of bondage. To state it plainly, I will reference the book; "This Life" by Martin Hagglund. Explaining spiritual freedom, he said, "In engaging the question 'what should I do?' We are also engaging the question 'who should I be?' And there is no final

---

[6] Christopher Dawson, "Religion and the Rise of Western Culture," in *Religion and the Rise of Western Culture* (New York, N.Y.: Image Books, 1991), pp. 62-62.

answer to that question."

Referencing the word liberty where freedom is the preferred word in the Garden,[7] the relationship of the man relative to all creation is addressed with two questions: "Who is man" and "Was he at liberty to recreate, particularly himself?" We have been taught to consider as good for life, the prohibition rather than the liberty of permission; Liberty being above even Life and Death for the power of both are within him. Using the phrase, "You are free to eat" rather than you have "liberty to eat" from every tree reveals the mind of the interpreter rather than the actual Word of God. The interpreter has deceived us because he himself had knowledge of the idea of being bound which Adam did not. Adam did not have use for, neither understood "free" for he never apprehended the distinction revealed only after he, as Jesus was portrayed to have been crucified, was portrayed as haven fallen. God gave man dominion and liberty and did not take this away with the prohibition; "you must not eat", he was able to eat from every tree but not every tree was beneficial for Life![8] Paul, in reference to this illustration goes on to ask, "why is my liberty judged of another man's conscience?" To gain the full of Paul's message, we must first consider the word conscience and its

---

[7] Genesis 2:16
[8] 1 Corinthians 10:23

etymology: "knowledge within oneself, sense of right and wrong, a moral sense, be (mutually) aware; be conscious of wrong."

For too long, what has been known of the world and Adam in the world has been made known from the consciousness of man's; fear of living made known by knowledge of the prohibition. The interpretation of the Word of God by a man who is prohibited by his own fearful knowledge of himself is not enough to navigate for others The Holy Writ of God. Man has proliferated the doctrine of fear and death disguised himself by the image of the Serpent who speaks with a religious tongue, the lie: Man is not the Image and Likeness of God and formed a doctrine which further disarms the Man of his Divine Birthright and permission to See himself as does God.

"What you see when you look at something depends not so much on what is there as on the assumption you make when you look." Your assumptions determine not only what you see but also what you do, for they govern all your conscious and subconscious movements towards the fulfillment of themselves.[9]

Man has become not who he believes himself to be but

---

[9] Neville, *The Power of Awareness* (New York: Tarcher Perigee, 2012),30.

rather "what" not who the Serpent has told him he is. The 23rd Psalm of David is exceedingly popular, possibly one of the most popular but is it the reality of the individual who wrote it or does his life experiences and failures exemplify the experience of the one who accepts David's state of spiritual turmoil and trouble as "The Gospel"? Verses 4-6 says, "yea though I walk through the Valley of the Shadow of Death"! Ask yourself a few questions… Did God create the Valley of the Shadow of Death? Or did disobedience, not Adam's disobedience but David's gave him his experience and your decisions create yours. We experience the Valley through perception and not necessarily reality, certainly not God's expectation and reality for his Son. The Valley and Death comes for identification and resurrection! The experiences come not to stay but only if you the Image of God say Let It Be!

The aim of this book is twofold: to identify God's Rest setting free Convoluted Man: the 2nd Adam and to reveal a mystery: There is only One! The soul who has been given liberty to eat has been given freedom for sure but is also charged with restraint. Man has the freewill to partake of all that is offered in this world and could not practice uninhibited liberty without the freedom to eat the prohibited fruit. It is the belief in Good against Evil that has formed the foundation of all three of the major religions: God who is but one Spirit not only battles the spirit of wickedness, but His creation must also enter battle with a malevolent spirit. A malevolent spirit? How, if God is One? Religion fails however to identify how evil could come from a Holy Nature acting on nothingness and how One Holy Nature could have an enemy in "His world". Who created this Valley, this Great Paradox? These two Wombs; Eve and Mary. This great paradox is the result of man's awareness of his own evil inclination who then attempts to identify its origin as outside himself; The man who cannot control himself blames his environment not realizing that the environment is himself, the atmosphere is his space.

It has been said by one of the greatest minds of the 20th Century, James Allen, "As a Man Thinketh, So Is He."
Meaning that man is not because 'he was', but that 'he is' because he believed. This book is for those who have been searching for the truth but have been told a lie. What lie? That man is weak, fragile, and wicked. The world has been deceived and because of his belief, man has manifested another creation, a creation in which death and sickness has dominion. Let us take this scripture as an example for what man thinks of himself. Psalm 82:6, "I said, "You are gods; you are all sons of the Highest. And then Psalm 8:4-6, *"What is man that You remember him, the son of man that You look after him? You made him*

little less than God and crowned him with glory and honor. You made him lord over the works of Your hands; You put everything under his feet; **Authority**." We are not waiting on everything to be placed under his feet and neither is a greater one to come than the Adam made in God's Image.

Again, creation is not waiting on the ruler of the earth, according to Genesis 1:26, the ruler to whom all authority was given was none other than the Man whom God had created. Adam practiced his authority when he named all the creatures. To name means to decide according to the nature of. I ask the question, who knows the nature except the Creator who gave the image to the Man enabling him to make the distinction, identifying all that exists in his world. (He alone creates his environment) Man is not weak, man is not fragile, man is the manifestation of God calling into existence those things which do exist affecting the quality of his own existence. In this case, Man is Lord over the works of God's hands. (Psalm 8:6) It is difficult for the fallen man to perceive himself as one crowned with Glory. What Glory, the same Glory that was given to Christ. (John 17:22) Man was given that same Glory at the beginning of the world. That Glory does not have to come, that Glory must be realized. This book is designed to challenge and define your vision so that you may realize the Glory of God in you… The Glory of God is you!

ADAM Man Convoluted but GOD

Christ did not have his life taken from him, he laid down his life. The enemy did not take away the life God gave the Man, the **Enemy Is The Man** who cannot perceive the Spirit of God in himself, therefore he is not alive for he laid down his Glorious Life for the Lesser. This is Evil; he who does not know himself, is the only evil which exists, for it is impossible to know God if the self that is known is dead. God in Man produces the wholeness of being. God made him whole, the enemy made him lack, not physically but perverted his conception of himself. Who then is The Enemy of Man? How did the Snake Speak? With Human or with Ophidian Lips?

The same is promulgated today in the Western Theology, in the form of The Original Sin Doctrine. The doctrine that causes man to believe that they: the man and his nature(wife) are inherently evil although their inheritance is from God. Some argue in support of this doctrine armed with Psalm 51:5 to prove that which God has blessed and called good has been since conception, "sin". They do this without 1st Context, 2nd Content, and 3rd Thought or Thoth, respective to equilibrium and balance in their interpretation and apologetics. In other words, the failure to remember Ma'at in their Hermeneutics. David's 51st Psalm was in response to a feeling of conviction for cogitating lustful thoughts in his adolescence. (**Uriah**) His thoughts of adultery crystalized into adulthood, a devoted and loyal Husband murdered. The man does not kill or sacrifice the son of perdition but leads to the front line, to the fiercest point of battle the righteous man: The Christ to be Crucified. Uriah: Yah Is Light, to murder Uriah is to **Extinguish The Light Within...**

However, Psalm 51:5 does not support the idea of original sin and neither does David allude that conclusion. He speaks from condemnation, not as a righteous man! See conditions and circumstances and understand verse 3 of the same Psalm: "For I am conscious of my rebellion." HCSB To be conscious of rebellion is the effect of a temporary condition revealed by the circumstance: Guilt. David is not speaking for humanity but for his own struggle with sin, he is in this moment disconnected from I AM just as Adam was asked the question; "Where are you?" So is the divine man hidden in sin and cannot speak as the Son but as the adversary who uttered to the conscious of the man, you need to gratify your stomach is their god; their glory is in their shame. Philippians 3 They are focused on earthly things, and the adversary is the false belief! What God has joined, no man can change but is at liberty to live a lie and see himself as a sinner and die to receive Life. Enemy! You are an Oxymoron! I AM, Come! Come! I AM so that I can have Life and Life With Abundance. Let me see that the World is my Garden, the world in which I live is the **Circum**stance of What I Have Believed! A man's thoughts are his Orbit, get it? **Circulus where I stand!** Geometry's elliptical revolution: distances of each point in its **periphery** from two fixed points: As far as he has Vision, he has reality. Adam, how do you see yourself?

Until men can sit down with other men and have an unprejudiced conversation about God, we will never be able to contemplate and worship one brought together in Truth. Is there any wonder why the ancient Semitic people of the desert viewed and served Yahweh as they did? Imagine that you were traveling through the desert being scorched by the desert heat, desiring food but unable to grow crops to sustain the number of people **traveling** with you. The story comes from a Nomad, they did not know from where they came and the image of God as a relentless, moody, and vengeful Monarch who occasionally showed favor when the man He created offered a sacrifice to appease Him was their God.

(Think about what you are thinking about when you believe in sacrificing anything except yourself)

Let us take on the other hand, the Canaanites who dwelt in the land of milk and honey. They viewed El as a God of mercy and blessings who was mostly merciful and gracious to them but sometimes revealed His hand of judgement.

Consider the behavior and religion of both peoples based on the yielding of the land. One group considered themselves the chosen of God because their fields always produced, allowing them to celebrate with lavish orgies and drunkenness. The Nomad on the other hand celebrated God in their strict customs and ceremonies forming two forms of worship of the same Creator according to their **periphery**. Let Us stop living in the shadows of another man's mind and his insufficiencies. Let Us stop living in the Valley, a Shadow of what God has given and desired for Man. Let Us stop looking to man for answers that only God has. When we eat from Man's Garden... his Valley... his Reality, we are truly walking in the Valley of the Shadow of Death!

The purpose of this book is to bring harm to the man who cannot See! Realizing the darkness, He may search for the Light...

Before going further into the reading of this book, you must understand a particularly important concept... If you gain nothing else, get this #1 Principle (which all else clings) firmly fixed in your mind! The Kingdom of God Is Within You!

What does that really mean? I will only give a definition and allow you to conceptualize in your own mind its implications. **Kingdom:** the realm in which God's will is fulfilled. **Realm:** a royal jurisdiction or extent of government.

ADAM Man Convoluted but GOD

You are the Royal jurisdiction where God's will is fulfilled... The only way to cease being you, let me say it again, the only way to stop being who you are, is to be unmade. If you want to become someone else, you must lose your mind (**Moses**). To stop existing as the person you are, to stop the experience you are presently experiencing; you must lose the former mind or old way of thinking and get the mind that God recommends for you (**Moses**). If you want God to use; exhibit, manifest the divine Self through you (**Moses**), You must be willing to Get Lost to old habits! You must be willing to get caught up in a new state of consciousness! (**Moses**) You must be willing to be wrapped up in the new life desired (**Christ**), you must be willing to be stripped naked (**Christ**), you must be willing to walk around naked, you must be willing to take off the clothes of the old man (**Adam**) and dress up with the mind of (**Christ**) you must be willing to be undressed...

And He Clothed Them!

If you want to accomplish something greater, you must stop being the old you. Stop being you and become someone else and then and only then will your world change.

Seize the moment... Christ told his disciples in terms and a language that those of his time could relate: "Work while it is day" I know that you are a different people of a different time and have wondered what it means to work while it is day.

I wondered about it myself. I know you have been waiting to hear it in a language of which you can relate, I know you are saying to yourself; "if I could understand this saying, I COULD DO MORE WORK", well here it is: You have been given a moment and a plot of land to work!

Stop waiting until you die to live! Live like you are already Alive.

Now, do you see it? Seize the moment! Christ told his disciples to seize the moment! Let me be honest with you, this life is the only moment you are going to get. This plot of land right where you are is the only land you are going to get (**Moses**). Take your shoes off and live. The only way you get out of this land is by death. Ask Adam, he died, and God put him out. I know you do not understand: This plot of land given to you, the situation that you are in, therein lies your blessing. Right under you (**Moses take your shoes off**), the ground where you are is Holy Ground! You are not going to get another plot of land. Get it; PLOT: God has already outlined a path for you, it is the reason you were placed in your garden; to work the land, manipulate the situation, outsmart adversity. YOU'RE BIGGER THAN THAT! Everything you face, is presenting itself to make you aware of the available resources. (**Power**) Outside of you? No! The Power of God in You (**Christ**)... I know, you do not understand. Listen, the earth is waiting in eager expectation for the children of God to be revealed. (The Earth, **Mother** Earth with all her vicissitudes (**opportunity**) is Nurturing you! The situation which has the appearances of evil/trouble is nothing but your destiny, (God took the man and placed him in a Garden to feed him) God told your destiny to rise and say to you, "Until you rule me, I will appear as chaos" (**Remember in the beginning, God Spoke to Chaos?**) Chaos: The Ancient Dragon, goddess of the Sea…

Mr. Minister! I do not believe this stuff you are preaching! Everything you say is **unorthodox to my indoctrination**! *Show us proof for what you say!*

Turn with me to Genesis: God told Cain the enemy is crouching at your door… what door? The same door to your destiny. He, God said but you must master it. If you do not, it will stop you…

The appearance of, <u>Appearance of</u>… an image of! … An Illusion will stop you! What illusion?… The serpent in the Tree!

Then He told Moses who now had a New Mind, get back to Egypt and FACE <u>your enemy.</u> (**Serpent**) With a New Mind (**Christ**) and a different perspective of… not of the enemy but of himself. (**Burning Bush**)

God revealed the man to Himself, and they Saw God

speak to the Sea! But their eyes saw Moses...

Hopefully, the reader can understand the principle involved in the above; The environment effects the thoughts of those who dwell in it. To get freed from the environment, change the way you think about the environment. If your environment is undesirable, dwelling on the state of the present condition, reinforces that condition. Your personality is but a collection of experiences believed to be true. Belief in past experiences negative or positive effect what you believe about the future. Collective thoughts multiplied by time create the State of Being of the individual. **(Atmosphere)** Since your personality is affected by experiences, and what you believe about these experiences influences how you perceive reality, the first principle to grasp here is; Your Personality creates your Personal Reality, and your personal reality is the space in which you live.

What has Egypt to do with the introduction of this book and with the Bible? God sent Moses away from his familiar environment to get acquainted with a different self. It was not for Moses to find God at the burning bush but that he should find himself and when he found himself, he found God... Once he saw God within himself, he changed his environment. Moses, born a Hebrew not only lived in Egypt for a portion of his life but according to Acts 7:20-24, he became a member of Pharaoh's household and was educated in all the wisdom of the Egyptians. "At that time Moses was born, and he was no ordinary child. For three months he was cared for by his family. When he was placed outside, Pharaoh's daughter took him and brought him up as her own son. Moses was educated in all the wisdom of the Egyptians and was powerful in speech and action. Notice that here Moses is described as **Powerful In Speech** concerning Egyptian Education and Wisdom but was afraid to even speak to the Israelites according to Exodus 4:10, "I am not eloquent, either in the past or since you have spoken to your servant, but I am slow of speech and of tongue." (Hebrew history and language)

When Moses were forty years old, he decided to visit his own people, the Israelites. He saw one of them being mistreated by an Egyptian, so he went to his defense and avenged him by killing the Egyptian".[10] Educated in all the wisdom of the Egyptians, Moses at the age of 40 fled to the land of the Midianites where he married the daughter of a Midianite Priest and remained according to the book of Acts 7:30 for 40 more years as a member of Jethro's household.

---

[10] All Biblical quotations taken from HCSB unless otherwise noted. "Acts 7:20-24"

Returning to Egypt for the last 40 years of his life to lead the children of Israel out of "Egypt", the land of bondage or the campus where Moses obtained his spiritual degree. This author has been living in America for 46 years and within this 46-year period, has become familiar with the culture of America, mainly its laws, music, religion, foods, and language. The fashion in which I think, speak, and act, represents the culture of which I relate. It is proper to emphasize the fact that those who penned the Bible were humans, conditioned mentally be it consciously or unconsciously by interaction with others of the genus, Adam. It is my intention to direct attention to the fact that although Moses was born a Hebrew, his culture was that of an Egyptian by his inherited status; "grandson" of the ruling Egyptian Pharaoh. Moses as the historian of the Pentateuch could not have possessed the religious orthodoxies of the modern Christian or Jew in relation to divinely inspired scripture. Therefore, we should understand that at least a portion of what we know today as "Torah" given by God was filtered through the mind of Moses the Egyptian rather than Moses the Hebrew or Jew.

In relation to this point of view, David M. Howard referencing Younger, Carr and Bebbington states, "Geschichte is an account of past events in terms of their contemporary significance and should be understood as essentially referring to the essence of what is historical, as penetrated by the mind of the historian."[11] Furthermore, John Dewey an American philosopher and educator from the mid-1800's states,

"I believe that all education proceeds by the participation of the individual in the social consciousness of the race. This process begins unconsciously almost at birth, and is continually shaping the individual's powers, saturating his consciousness, forming his habits, training his ideas, and arousing his feelings and emotions. Through this unconscious education the individual gradually comes to share in the intellectual and moral resources which humanity has succeeded in getting together. He becomes an inheritor of the funded capital of civilization. The most formal and technical education in the world cannot safely depart from this general process."[12]

Moses' race and social consciousness, influenced in the same manner as modern men subjugated to any ruling class and or civilization must reflect according to Dewey in the person's ideas, emotions, and habits. Dewey further states in his creed,

"I believe that the only true education comes through the stimulation of the child's powers by the demands of the social situations in

---

[11] David M. Howard, *An Introduction to the Old Testament Historical Books* (Chicago: Moody Press, ©1993), 45-46.

[12] http://infed.org/mobi/john-dewey-my-pedagogical-creed/. Retrieved:11/28/2017.

which he finds himself. Through these demands he is stimulated to act as a member of a unity, to emerge from his original narrowness of action and feeling, and to conceive of himself from the standpoint of the welfare of the group to which he belongs. Through the responses which others make to his own activities he comes to know what these mean in social terms. The value which they have is reflected into them. For instance, through the response which is made to the child's instinctive babblings the child comes to know what those babblings mean; they are transformed into articulate language and thus the child is introduced into the consolidated wealth of ideas and emotions which are now summed up in language."[13]

That which is of utmost importance to the understanding of this author's perspective and purpose for writing this book is that Moses the Egyptian left a message for the spiritual man who could see beyond the literal interpretation, receiving the spirit of the message, allowing ancient Egyptian and other ANE theology as his sources to reveal the deeper meanings of Biblical truth. In his spiritual writings, Moses revealed the meaning of resurrection known only by the elect, the resurrection of the Eternal Soul (Baby Jesus), hidden from the religious man since the foundation of the earth but found by a man who called a nation out of the sea. This brief Biblical criticism as used here should not

---

[13] http://infed.org/mobi/john-dewey-my-pedagogical-creed/. Retrieved: 11/28/2017.

discourage the true seeker and has only been used to aid in the identification of the origin from which the writings of the Bible were produced, and what influences were at work in the mind of one of its most important writers. It has become vividly clear that until man began to think for himself, rather than accepting blindly what was written, he assumed the role of a child (neophyte), afraid to ask the questions who, what or why I believe. While seeking diligently for the truth, it often happens that discovering the truth involves experiencing pain. Perceived only because he who earnestly seeks truth has been internally motivated by questions about a "Learned" truth.

For so many years and for so many children of faith, to examine truth has been viewed as a lack of faith. To the contrary of this heresy, truth which endures after it has been thoroughly unpacked, produces the faith we long for. Faith in what one does not genuinely believe produces within the individual "Cognitive Dissonance" and this battle in the mind has caused the psychosis of which Paul expressed when he said and is quoted without understanding by many spiritual leaders,

"For I do not understand what I am doing, because I do not practice what I want to do, but I do what I hate. And if I do what I do not want to do, I agree with the law that it is good. So now I am no longer the one doing it, but it is sin living in me."

It is not sin living in you, it is someone else living

through you! The one who does not live according to what he believes, does not have the courage to Live and the one who lives the life of another does not have life at all. Again, he who does not have the courage to live the life in which he believes is an "Invisible Man" and a man who is invisible is defined by the one who created him. It is impossible for others to "see in you" what you do not "See In Yourself". This book is for those who for years have allowed others to "See in You" what you have not seen in yourself. Those who are not me have defined me! They have poured in me a lie which has caused myself to disappear. The life I have lived, has been for their benefit, their good fortune perpetuated by the lie they told me, has created heaven for them and hell for me…

There is nothing wrong with you!

If there is something wrong with you, it is only because of this one reason… I will tell you the reason later but first I must conclude this introduction.

Some believe the words of Moses have been edited, if the words of Moses have been edited at all, it was committed by those who could not understand the spiritual messenger; Moses the Egyptian does not represent the physical ethnicity of the man. Moses the Egyptian represents so many of us to whom our true selves have been at first hidden but now are being revealed. Let me explain. When we use the expression;

"Others only see in you what you see in yourself", we have to first ask the question; how does someone else first of all "see in me"? When you allow someone the authority to see in you, do you really realize the psychological ramifications of such a demoralizing act? Before someone can Penetrate you, there must first be an Orifice, there must first be a space that is hollow! Who Is He That Has Emptied You Adam and Eve? To be continued…

Let There Be Light...

"The deeper the slumber and degree of contentment in darkness; the more troublesome the Light of Instruction." The Minister

The Spirit of God was hovering over the surface of the waters and life was made. Therefore, Man was also made full of the same Life, it must be Manifested through him...

This chapter is introduced with an explanation, an exegesis of the word Light; Genesis 1:3 Let there be dawn (the period immediately between day and night ignorance and wisdom) known and the unknown. The dawn of the ability to be known by perceiving... Perception does not exist without contrast. Contrast is not a word unless the light illuminates the darkness... The beginning of perceiving the brilliance of God's mind. The light is God and God is light, the light has always been... But The Light is impossible to perceive without Revelation: the knowledge of God. Those things created first had to have been created with the ability to perceive the works and plan of God, and were therefore able to give light, the sustaining light of life. God said "Be" the words "let there" are only clarifying words used to quantify the Being who came forth from the command... Meaning, that which becomes, came from you!

In the beginning, God gave permission to the intelligence of sustainable life, He put Life in everything He Created. Dawn: The beginning of the appearance of the Son, he must become apparent to the mind. Although the Sun is the light, without the faculty of sight, even that light is darkness. Let there Be Cain and Abel... God created Able/Abel = The Ability to see, not with the eyes but the Spiritual light. Possibility and perception preceded the physical life: Cain. Listen; The Lord had regard for Abel. (Genesis 4:4)

Abel Knew God and was Known by Him. Ignorance Killed Abel and Cain's world became dark and cold for he walked in the land of Nod; a land not inhabited by the Children of God... Ignorance is the cause of life's troubles. The word regard means: "take notice of" Abel God Knew, for Abel according to his deeds was led by the righteous light. Abel was known by God because God took notice not of Abel's life but of the Light of the World, the Abel/Indwelling Son in man, the light enabled him to see! Can you See? Abel's ability to make manifest that which was in him gave him life; that Infinite

Potential of Man. I am going to stop right here; I'm going too deep! Before we begin to journey further beneath the surface, let us identify abstract thought from concrete thought and then we may walk side by side.

It has been said that before two can argue the difference of opinion, there must be a common source of reference. The reference then is The Beginning, and the beginning began "In The Light".

Christ loaded his disciples into a single boat to illuminate the Spirit of Life who dwells below the chamber of sub consciousness within each of them and all of us to deluge them into a spiritual quickening which would trouble the waters of this dark world (Matthew 8:23-27). From the darkness of nothingness and from the darkness of the storms of life comes the light; if only Adam would take a stance in the positioning of God's discipline he would perceive that from every dark storm or condition in which he endures emerges a student of the condition: fashioned by perseverance, the man becomes Lord of his character, who is then able to speak through faith to the condition so that the perceived obstacle will become the instrument by which he is elevated to **Sonship**. The Son becoming a vessel for the deliverance of those who have been blinded by their own storms of indulgence. Their Own Indulgences, because "We Create What We Live In." Bold enough to create for himself if they do not exist, his own conditions, the conditions which are progressively creating for him in perfection, his desired future… (see Jeremiah 29:11)

This in similitude to the evolving Adam who travels through spheres of life leaving one circle of experience, advancing to the next, the new soul of the advancing Adam has all the knowledge of the old indulgences but is no longer restricted by the darkness of ignorance which led to the confined chambers of his own destructive thought:

"The Divine Essence leaving a Golden Box to dwell In the Son; the end of a Paradigm, Man as the Son has begun."

Becoming Lord of the smaller sphere of conditions the new soul presses outwardly on all sides to new and larger circles leaving the small but able to return to lead out those confined by temporary space and time (what a predicament in Aristotelian logic?). The Adam who once was a slave has become the Son, The Son who becomes God?

"The life of the Adam is a self-evolving circle, which starts from a shell imperceptibly small like a mustard seed containing the limitless Breath of Light… the sol, the sawel, the soul, the son of man, the Christ" The Sun of Righteousness has arisen…_{The Minister}

Christ made his disciples aware of this inner light source of creation who can speak to the darkness of nothingness. Creating for himself that which is meaningful to himself, from which substance has been made. The light in all creation: the marvelous light who is the same light who existed in darkness, but the darkness did not comprehend because the light had not been revealed. Because the light had not been revealed, does not mean that the light did not exist. Since the Spirit is of perpetual existence so are the thoughts perpetually eternal and not evolving. The realization that the thoughts of The Creator do not evolve and are not constructed by trial and error is paramount to understanding the duality (does man really have dual natures) in the existence of Adam who came from the Eternal Mind but did not understand the psychology of dualism (mind & matter) of self because of the brilliance in the Oneness of the Master Mind. The light of the spiritual is now being revealed from the flesh that existed as darkness but only as darkness in the sense that matter or the self-had not been revealed as divided as in individualism. The light is not the creator but is the revelation of that which existed but was not yet understood for the Word had not yet been spoken… Man is the Faculty of the True Light…

Let us return to Concrete and Abstract thought; concrete thought defined: Concrete thinking is literal thinking made known or experienced by the five senses focused on the physical world. People engaged in concrete thinking are focused on facts in the here and now, physical objects, and literal definitions. An example of this type of thought expression used to show anger by one of the eastern authors of the Torah has been expressed in the Hebrew language as the flaring of the nostrils; and the symbolic expression of this same word anger is a bull with its nostrils flared open. Let us understand that for the written language to express an idea of communication, the symbol representing the word must first be understood. (Effective word, paints a picture) Therefore, one can read a word and derive its meaning but without understanding the idea which gave life to the symbol, one is as "sounding brass, or a tinkling cymbal." The symbol conveys unspoken spirit to the obedient mind sent by the progenitor of the thought which formed the symbol used to identify the condition of the heart the second what was written as word is eaten or consumed by the sheep and the goat. Do you perceive now the symbol of the sheep and goat? Both, the sheep, and the goat exist in the essence of man, separated, and identified by what the man consumes and becomes as a product of his consumption.

    The reader can be misled by what is written for what is written no longer belongs to the author but is received by the reader and is filtered through the mind of the beholder who if one's heart is not pure, cannot possibly extrapolate the meat of the symbol from watered down word; watered down because if any man should know Christ, they should come as a child, an un-Adult-terated mind who has not consumed that which was in the center of man's evil desire: The Tree of the Knowledge of this world. Abstract, on the other hand has a separate meaning defined as existing in thought or as an idea but not having a physical or concrete existence. If this book has intrigued you at all so far, it is the desire of The Minister that you, the neophyte (Pupil) are ready to set aside and separate yourself from indoctrinations which limit your spiritual growth and are beginning to understand the difference between concrete and abstract, and that the contrast between spirituality and religion which will be covered in a later chapter are also surfacing in the planes of your mind. There should also be a twinkling of light that is illuminating the contrast of faith birthed by spiritual apprehension rather than disbelief birthed from the absence of concrete proof.

"Abstract proof that is not supported by concrete substance or an animated object, can be made fully alive in the mind of the faithful whose hope is not in the physical but the One who transcends concrete understanding".

Hopefully, the Pupil is also understanding that it is not

the intent of The Minister to favor eastern thought: concrete over western thought: abstract. Rather, in the revelation of light being taken from darkness but the darkness did not understand, both concrete and abstract are relevant as will be made known shortly as you continue to read this book and as you continue the "Spiritual Journey of Life" which is intended to reveal to Adam the deepest darkness in creation; darkness in the sense of the mind of the Most High having not yet been revealed; not darkness meaning that nothing existed. For all that is being revealed has up to the time of the revealing existed; even if this existence had not yet been understood by those who would later explain the explosion of the Atom but not understand the <u>Light</u> which dwells in the Adam.

The ancients mastered the art of expressing light to the initiates of the wisdom schools of knowledge. Those endeavoring to or whom have been found worthy of receiving this knowledge were introduced to symbols and the understanding and meaning of symbolism which has the purpose of revealing secrets to the enlightened but to the thief who has robbed, ravaged and raped ancient peoples, caves and coffins, a religion of dead and powerless symbolism of which inanimate objects and deities are venerated and worshiped as God, the religion itself violating the commandment which forbade this type of false worship. The Minister says again; to those who only view such symbolism on a cave wall and then institute a Religion which worships symbols rather than the truth of which the symbols identify, these are the thieves or they of whom Christ spoke: Matthew 13:8-17. *Still other seed fell on good soil, where it produced a crop—a hundred, sixty or thirty times what was sown.* ⁹ **Whoever has ears, let them hear."**

¹⁰ *The disciples came to him and asked, "Why do you speak to the people in parables?"* ¹¹ *He replied,* **"Because the knowledge of the secrets of the kingdom of heaven has been given to you, but not to them.** ¹² *Whoever has will be given more, and they will have an abundance. Whoever does not have, even what they have will be taken from them.* ¹³ *This is why I speak to them in parables: "Though seeing, they do not see; though hearing, they do not hear or understand.* ¹⁴ **In them is fulfilled the prophecy of Isaiah: Isaiah 6:9-10** *"'You will be ever hearing but never understanding; you will be ever seeing but never perceiving.* ¹⁵ *For this people's heart has become calloused; they hardly hear with their ears, and they have closed their eyes. Otherwise, they might see with their eyes, hear with their ears, understand with their hearts and turn, and be healed.* ¹⁶ *But blessed are your eyes because they see, and your ears because they hear.* ¹⁷ *For truly I tell you, many prophets and righteous people longed to see what you see but did not see it, and to hear what you hear but did not hear it.*

(Moses, one of the authors of the Torah had this knowledge and delivered dual understandings from one Loaf of Bread, "His Face was Veiled" thus feeding the masses who possessed different understandings, purposes, motivations and even gods, identifying an esoteric knowledge revealed by those of whom it is said found him in the Nile River.)

Note: Bulrushes of the Nile and the infant Moses, could this have been the genesis of the evolution of the law of the world? Found by those who depended on the life in the Waters of the Nile River, who bathed in that life of the Nile and then received the revelation of life as the beginning of the Law.

The law is the key to life… One of the core myths of ancient Egypt concerned the gods Osiris, Isis, Seth, and Horus. Seth and Osiris were brother deities, Seth representing evil and chaos, Osiris representing good and fertility. The battle between the two resulted in the death of Osiris. Before he died Osiris could not impregnate his wife and sister Isis, goddess of wisdom and beauty. Isis in turn divinely became impregnated with the Good seed of Osiris and gave birth to Horus who is represented in Egyptian mythology (so called by invaders) as the falcon-headed god of kingship. When Seth learned that his brother Osiris's offspring had been born, he sought to kill the baby boy. Isis prepared a basket of reeds to hide him in the marshland of the Nile Delta, where she suckled him and protected him, along with the watchful eye of her sister,

Nephthys, from the **Snakes**, scorpions, and other dangerous creatures until he grew and prospered. One of the keys to understanding the light of the creation and the brilliance of this myth is to understand that goodness and righteousness was personified by the god Osiris and Chaos personified by Seth who wanted to kill the seed of Osiris. When it says, "the seed of Osiris, or that which Wisdom (Isis) and Righteousness (Osiris) produces", the "Seed" becomes the object of Seth's rage. The Minister now requests that the neophyte reflect on Genesis 3:15 of the KJV. So, ask yourself; what does righteous wisdom produce? The Minister will only give a hint: if wisdom comes from God or is the seed of God and the pupil is impregnated and permeated by this seed of God, who then will he See in Himself?... Not who man say you are... Is the light shining yet?

The creation waits in eager expectation for the revelation of the sons of God. Berean Study Bible Romans 8:19

Who is really being spoken of in this Egyptian myth used to express an esoteric understanding to those who can hear what the spirit is revealing to the churches? Until who grew and prospered? Baby Jesus in You... Should those enlightened see the parallel of Mary and Christ? Those who view the scriptures as literal see the birth of the baby Christ as a beautiful nativity scene worthy of display to show pious worship of the birth of the Savior. But few have been enlightened to perceive the brilliant light of the hidden word which permeates this physical event. The infant *(The Light)* was coming into the world but could only come through a virgin heart *(Mary)*. There was not any room in the Inn *(Materialistic proud heart)* for this Light to be birthed. Not coming through the aristocracy of the world, wisdom emanates from the humble heart unsoiled by the garments of flesh *(manmade religion)* which prevents the manifestation of the true Light that created the world. Or should we simply hear the words of Isaiah conveying wisdom, spoken of as Horus in This Egyptian parable has been hidden from the world because their hearts were perverted. Mary has been portrayed as the virgin Isis who personifies the sanctity of the virgin who has opened the door of her heart to the Giver of the Wisdom buried in the foundation of the world.

Solomon expresses it thusly: Wisdom has built her house; she has set up its **_seven pillars._** She has prepared her meat and mixed her wine; she has also set her table. She has sent out her servants she calls from the highest point of the city, "Let all who are simple come to my house!" To those who have no sense she says, "Come, eat my food, and drink the wine I have mixed. Leave your simple ways and you will live; walk in the way of insight." Whoever corrects a mocker invite insults: whoever rebukes the wicked incurs abuse. <u>Do not rebuke mockers or they will hate you;</u> **rebuke the wise and they will love you.** Instruct the wise and they will be wiser still; teach the righteous and they will add to their learning.

<u>***The fear of the Lord is the beginning of wisdom,***</u> ***and knowledge of the Holy One is understanding. For through wisdom your days will be many, and years will be added to your life. If you are wise, your wisdom will reward you; if you are a mocker, you alone will suffer.***

The Minister has now introduced you to a motif of ancient literature known by scholars and students of seminary alike as "The Exposed Infant Motif". In this motif, the heroic child (neophyte) often the child of a god or one who themselves is to become a god must face nature and the dangerous creatures there of before divinity is bestowed and the Child becomes a god or God. Now, the pupil may understand the difference between concrete and abstract more clearly, also seeing the origin and history of influence on the Greek author of Romans 8:19 above. And again, in Romans, the author says, "For the creation was subjected to frustration, not by its own choice, but by the will of the one who subjected it, in hope that the creation itself will be liberated from its bondage to decay and brought into the freedom and glory of the **Children of God**. We know that the whole creation has been groaning as in the pains of childbirth right up to the present time". Romans 8:20-22

God fabricated an enemy in the foundation of creation by which the children would reign. This the Light of creation; the light which comes from darkness, the mind of man. Let us take a look...

"Fabricate; according to www.merriam-webster.com, means to invent, create; to make up for the purpose of deception. Construct, manufacture; specifically: to construct from diverse and usually standardized parts."

Why would The Minister associate a definition that attaches deception to an existence created from nothing, Good or Bad for neither existed? To reveal the mind of man, light and darkness, man divided against himself, the word Glorify must be mentioned. **There is no Glorification without Identification.** The premature first Adam (man in infancy, a neophyte), the man who frustrated creation, represents in form the whole man and at once, the spiritual man not yet glorified; darkness was in the world. The second dispensation of the man Adam after eating from the (table of wisdom, Isaiah 50:4-7) made known the once hidden in darkness, the glorified man.

When a child is born into this world, he must go

through a series of vaccinations. Because of the atmosphere of this world, according to the Centers for Disease Control, every child must be inoculated: *treat (a person or animal) with a vaccine to produce immunity against a disease. Introduce* **(an infective agent)** *into an organism.* CDC says, "Infants are particularly vulnerable to infectious diseases; that is why it is critical to protect them through immunization. Each day, nearly 12,000 babies are born in the United States who will need to be immunized before age two against 14 vaccine-preventable diseases. Immunizations help prevent the spread of disease and protect infants and toddlers against dangerous complications. **Immunization is one of the most important things a parent can do to protect their children's health.**"

When a soul is born into this world, it is vulnerable to 14 different diseases! In the mind of the primitive or those who have been spiritually quickened, one might say 14 different baleful (Baal) spirits.

With the introduction of an infective agent into the potentially susceptible host, the healthy immune system will generate antibodies against the disease or baleful spirit so that when the two finally meet in the center (a point, pivot, axis, etc., around which anything rotates or revolves) of the Garden of Eden; (which does not represent a physical place as much as it does a pivotal point of growth, transformation, liberation and the genesis of evolution for the traveler of light), Adam would be victorious because they are aware of this type of baleful presence. So, God Fabricated means God has Inoculated His Children…

The first Adam represents infancy or the genesis of the man in his process of evolution and God is his parent. Every creature perpetuates its kind to avoid extinction, mankind is not the exception. This is not a divine mystery, it is a natural process and is the plan of the Creator who says, "For this is what the Lord says, he who created the heavens, he is God; he who fashioned and made the earth, he founded it; **he did not create it to be empty but formed it to be inhabited.**" Isaiah 45:18. Now that we have understood that this earth was not created to be destroyed as some would have you believe. Now that we also understand that perpetual life is the intent of its Creator then it is also safe to deduce that the earth has been formed with life giving "subjective substance" and healing set in its foundations. What is this indwelling source of life? The Light: Righteousness, Wisdom, Understanding, Balance and Love… These are the Creators of the World (Personified as One Godhead Elohim); the True Light who was in the world, but darkness could not comprehend. These are they who said, "Let Us Make Man in Our Image", man the expression of Light. In the absence of light, images are not seen; in the absence of light, man's awareness of himself is obscured; in the absence of physical light, the righteous will be the light of the world.

You have been made subject to darkness so that God may be identified in you! You have been made subject to darkness so that the light in you will illuminate the darkness! You have been made subject to darkness so that you may be like God who formed the light of reality from nothingness. Where is your God if all you see is darkness? For those living in darkness, a light has dawned, a Great light is now being seen: God said to Moses, "See, I have made you like God to Pharaoh". Why has this darkness befallen you? For those who have ears, let them apprehend what the Spirit is saying, let those who are the children of God rejoice in their darkest hour! For in your darkest hour, God has blessed you to be like Him forming your own reality. (Darkness in the sense of Infinite Potential not yet revealed) **Christ…** Shape your reality from darkness, God created you in His image and blessed you with darkness so that He could dwell in you and you in Him. Speak to your darkness because **Man is** the **infest**ation of God on earth. Did you get that? Man is God **manifest.** Let the Minister explain: **Infest**- *to be numerous in, as anything undesirable or* **_troublesome._** Before The Divine Spirit troubled darkness, the earth was covered by darkness for those who could not see the potential of Life. How did He trouble darkness? It is simple, He subjected Himself in Man who is the manifestation of God on earth. What is another word like infest? Let us reflect on

ADAM Man Convoluted but GOD

Genesis. God said to man, "be fruitful and multiply" multiply who? More of my Essence… Another word for infest but with a positive denotation is impregnate. The carnal mind perceives what the flesh desires and only comprehends what is common to him: Sex between Adam and Eve, but the Spirit makes it clear that the words multiply and fruitful means to create a God permeated life on earth. Adam was to impregnate his wife (Eve- who represents the creative power; Desire of Man) with the divine seed of God.

Let me clarify the relation between Eve and desire: Success begins with Desire. If one is to be great, his greatness begins with a deep overwhelming desire to do or to become. Eve, the mother of all the living, sprang forth from the man's desire to create and without the mother of all that lives, his seed would have fallen to the ground and died for thought must be coupled with substance, thought needs to manipulate, thought must affect matter if change is to occur. (Mind over Matter) Man's purpose on earth is to replenish the earth by planting good seed back into the earth, the good seed of the Knowledge of God. The mystery: God spoke to Adam concerning man's Liberty on earth, in turn man was to be husband of his desire Eve, who if left to wander throughout the Garden of Eden alone or without wisdom, brings shame rather than Glory. (Ego, Id & Superego) Each man is made or unmade by his thoughts. The fallen Adam and Eve represents the dualism of the Tree of the Knowledge of Good and Evil. They became that which they ate and continued to replenish the earth with this perpetual seed of disobedience. Since they believed the Serpent, they were the first to perceive the serpent's mentality, they in essence, became the Serpent and shared its fate:

How you have fallen from heaven, morning star, son of the dawn! You have been cast down to the earth, you who once laid low the nations. You said in your heart, "I will ascend to the heavens; I will raise my throne above the stars of God; I will sit enthroned on the mount of assembly, on the utmost heights of Mount Zaphon. I will ascend above the tops of the clouds; I will make myself like the Most High." Notice it says, "make myself", Adam/Lucifer did not say, "I will be like God", to say, I will be, is not rebellious to the decree of God but rather is aligned with the decree; "Let us make man in our image". When man creates a righteousness for himself, he then represents the Serpent in the dualism of man. To be is to exist in the I Am who was identified to Moses in Moses's desert experience. To make for yourself is divination because to make outside of God's Law implies that there is the existence of an authority outside of God. There does exist an authority outside of God known as Death for there is no darkness in God. You have been made subject to the darkness of death to reveal God to those who are dead. Death does not have authority over the children on whom the light has dawned because the children on whom the light has dawned the message of Christ.

Light: *Hebrew (ôwr); pronounced ore. Defined: to be luminous; to make luminous. The light of creation was not given to create but to illuminate existence itself. The light was given to make manifest those things existing from everlasting in the mind of God of which darkness covered. The light reveals the wisdom of God. Because the light illuminates, it is the perception of the soul upon whom the light shines which determines the life in the light. What you see is the result of the hidden thought, every man's experiences are the ripened fruit of his own vineyard, he alone is the maker of himself.*

Sight does not take place in the eyes but in the mind, the eyes respond to the light, bending and refracting the light but it is the mind that paints the picture of reality and to this picture, the body responds as if the "mental picture" is reality. Be careful on what you allow your eyes to focus. If you are not in agreement with the contents of this book, put it down because what you see, gets into your soul, ever wondered why the eyes are pea shaped or in the shape of a seed? Your eyes are like a window to your soul, a germinating seed that takes root in your soul and permeates the being until he becomes that which he associates.

Remember the man, woman, serpent, and the tree. They became a product of all that they desired fueled by what their eyes saw. Their eyes responding to a false realization of a heaven painted by the serpent. (Heaven, where lives the Dead)... God gave us Life.

Every man's LOC, Level of Consciousness being the result of what he perceives. You are made aware of only those things that can be envisioned by you. Every eye is a pupil able to focus according to the light of which it has been illumined, creating for him his world that they said God created Heaven and Hell. He is himself, as the physical man a pupil of the light, for the light within instructs the pupil. The man existing in the garden of his own mind. The pupil, a small but vital part of the eye is responsible for the ability of the eyes to look at those things which do appear.

The physiology of the pupil: *The pupil is an opening that lets light into your eye. Since most of the light entering your eye does not escape, your pupil appears black. In dim light, your pupil expands to allow more light to enter your eye. In bright light, it contracts. Your pupil can range in diameter from 1.5 millimeters (1/16th of an inch) to more than 8 millimeters (1/3 of an inch). Light detected by the retina of your eye is converted to* **nerve impulses** *that travel down the optic nerve. Some of these nerve impulses go from the optic nerve to the muscles that control the size of the pupil.* **More light creates more impulses**, *causing the* *muscles to close the pupil. Part of the optic nerve from one eye crosses over and couples to the muscles that control the pupil size of the other eye.*

"The light of the body is the eye: if therefore thine eye be single; thy whole body shall be full of light. But if thine eye be evil; thy whole body shall be full of darkness. If therefore the light that is in thee be darkness, how great is that darkness! (Matthew 6:22-23)

Now we understand how a man is then divided within himself, when his vision is not single. We have read Moses killed the Egyptian, he was torn in two, the battle within Moses caused us to read but not understand Moses killed an Egyptian, the Egyptian was him…

The light shineth on all men without conscious effort of the man. This is the initial awakening/preparation for spiritual building. Let there be light (I Am the light of the world) Let there be light: the beginning of man's revelation of self and God. Most objects that absorb visible light release it as heat. So, although an object may appear dark, (Adam from the dark soil) He is likely bright at a frequency that carnal man cannot perceive. **STAY OPEN PUPIL AND LET IN THE LIGHT!**

Who quantified the darkness? God certainly did not make the entity darkness; he was a creation of the man. Darkness exists only in the absence of his presence! (How then does darkness and light dwell together?) Darkness advances only when light recedes. When darkness enters a room, it does not push light out. Darkness only exists where the light does not. God began creating while darkness covered everything. The (Light of Life) simply means the dawn of all that exists. Without that light nothing would exist is philosophical not spiritual for Nothingness never did exist, God Is! This is not basic to man's understanding of himself so, on your mark, get set, Live! To what does 1 John refer? (He), God is in the light? God did not exist to the man who himself was not known by God. Since God is according to 1 John; "In the Light", light being manifestation then God is the revelation of life, therefore, God is All in All and the only All is the light for darkness is the absence of life. Let there be light, the beginning of Life.

Man is indeed Living, moving and has His Being in the Mind of God for there is no other Thinker but God. What man can say that his thought is of a different substance than that which has first been known by God. Man creates within this life that has been made known. Darkness was not created for it is not a thing, true darkness (the darkness before life) only exists where light has not shown. However, the light is all and everything that exists does so because of the light of the life. There is no light in death, therefore death must remain unknown for if death is to be made known life would no longer exist; He must die and become someone else. Light was in the world shining in darkness, but the darkness understood it not. For when life is imaged, darkness ceases to exist. Man was afraid of the depths of the Sea, he was fearful of the ascension to heights of the stars, He was afraid of the darkness of the night, he therefore gave life to what he feared, Man made the unknown wicked for God only Knows and what God does not know, man fears; it therefore is his own imagination. Since God knows the deepest depths, and the highest heights, the darkness that man fears must then be from the lack of knowledge. Man personifies that which he does not understand: Evil defined… Thereby, giving life to a figment of imagination who can in man's mind, rival The One Spirit.

    In the light, man cannot comprehend darkness, to do so disturbs him. The question from the beginning; from where did man come and how came the dawn of first light? To answer this, we must begin with Man's perspective of the Light. 1) ***Perspective***: the art of drawing solid objects on a two 2) ***dimensional*** surface as to give the right 3) ***impression*** of their height, width, depth and 4) ***position*** in relation to each other when viewed from a particular point. Jesus asked the 5) ***fisherman,*** "Have you any 6) ***fish*** to 7) ***eat*** along with your 8) ***bread?***" The bread is a physical representation, a preparation of the mind to comprehend what they lacked. It was dark and they lacked fish: swim in the unknown waters of the mind, fish=ideas, eating fish= 9) **appropriation** of those ideas. The meaning of appropriation was first introduced to us by the eating from the tree in the garden. To appropriate the word of truth is to receive life from the 10) **substance** of the word. Jesus therefore spoke these spiritual words to the fisherman: **"You have bread, but you lack substance."** You have the word but to this point in your religious journey, the Spirit has not been your guide…

The true light which came into the world. Without this consciousness, although the world has always existed, could not have existed… For all things which do exist, was made manifest Through him all things were made. He alone is Consciousness. They got up, drove Him out of the town, and led Him to the **Brow of the hill on which the Town was Built,** *(their Church, religion) to throw Him over the cliff.* **But Jesus passed through the crowd and went on His way.** *Don't let the light pass through you… Understand the Light…*

The Day of the Lord...

Isaiah 55:10-11 "For as the rain or snow drops from heaven and returns not there, but soaks the earth, and make it bring forth **"vegetation, yielding seed"** *for sowing and bread for eating, So is the word that issues from My mouth: It does not come back to Me unfulfilled, But performs what I purpose, Achieves what I sent it to do."* (JPS Hebrew English TANAKH

Except that the Word accomplishes that which I please; **And make the thing whereto I sent it prosper.**

Many are the theory concerning the wording of the first clause of Genesis 1:1. Since we know that the Creator does not have a beginning; Well, let us pause to preface (the Creator does not have a beginning) because all who are reading this book do not have the same understanding of the Eternal Essence known as God by some Most High by others, Jehovah, Elohim and so forth is He praised for many of His presentations. All are not of the same religious influence, for all have come to know Him through diverse persuasions. What the neophyte should come to realize though is that translation of religious texts designed to reveal Him are the result of the influencing authority of the specific time, interpreted by an overseer; body or committee dedicated to the purpose of the accepted doctrine and understanding. Interpreters are not free men but are inhibited by the accepted paradigm. They are assigned a task and persuaded to think with limitation concerning what has already been accepted and outside of this limited thought, heresy you are to think only what you have been given to think. That man is in a controlled environment, what he produces has already been determined by those who created the environment, giving a false sense of freedom they foreknew what he would think. He who controls the Petri Dish, controls the growth within the Petri Dish.

What then does it mean, The Day of The Lord? Have you considered what it really conveys that God has a day? Because a thought is held in the mind, does not mean that the faculty of thought has been used to think. Therefore, if I say what I have been told to think, and the words that I speak create life then the life we are living if The Lord's Day, why so much talk about death? Have you ever considered what it would feel like to spend a day with The Lord? How long will that day be? There has been a shift of the Paradigm and instead of living in His day, Adam has died… A sign of a cross was given in the sky, look to the hills from where comes my help? Nay, my help comes not from the Sky. The King saw something in the **Sky**- c. 1200, "a cloud" from Old Norse sky, "cloud" "In hoc signo vinces", let the pupil apprehend what is not seen: Authoritative indoctrination of the Theology: (religious philosophy) of the cross.

In the biologist's lab there is what is known as the culture medium. This is the environment in which the development and behavior of a particular cell is observed. So, when you think about the day of the Lord, have you considered your own perspective, has your perspective been cultured? Listen, God has given us a cycle of evolution a cycle meaning a series of events established to transform the being from a simple to more complex form and all to be accomplished in a day, 70-man years or so. Such is the plan of the Creator that the man should be transformed from simple to complex or more precise, that he should become aware of his complexities revealed by the life given to him on God's Day… The Complexities of Man do not identify him as weak and sinful but to the contrary, God's Day reveals the complex form of the man, although he was in the world, the world knew him not for he was complex. The serpent said let us obscure the vision of the man and cause him to focus his attention not on this Day but on that which is beyond him. He will not be the ruler of Earth for we will make him gaze into the Clouds. Let me explain: Can any man by reading any religious book whatever his religious book may be and interpreting that book literally, not adding to it or reading into it words which do not exist, describe "heaven"? Why is it that man who has not mastered life on earth is so fascinated with life beyond the clouds? Why does he look for another day? Have you considered that maybe this alone is the day for you to Rule and the kings of this earth have created a different culture to obscure You, and take the good life away from you?

If Adam would have focused on how great he already was, would he have entertained the idea of another day? No, he would have identified the adversary and would **Stop Eating His Food.** So often we look for a change, so often we persuade ourselves that we have been planted in infertile ground but those who we consider blessed were planted in the best field. Maybe it is the culture in which you have been planted, maybe your people have been cursed and every other culture blessed with a Garden to work it and take care of it…

"In the beginning of God's creating, God who is neither male nor female but Spirit, decided to make known the essence of God through word that had not yet been known." For the sake of modern majority thought, the Minister will use the pronoun He; God decided to make himself known but first had to form matter as a conductor or conduit to receive and become that which is spoken so that His Word could become flesh. So, it is not God who has a beginning but His physical Word who was begotten or made alive and performed the creating. Alive does not mean that His Word was dead but that before the Word, nothing existed outside of His hovering Essence. The Creator of all sent His Word to the Earth to make it prosper and His Word made known the Earth to make known the Father for without the Earth, the Father was not known… But the pronoun He does not make God a man…

The word says, "Wisdom has built <u>her</u> house; <u>she</u> has set up its ***seven pillars.***"

On the **first pillar** of God's plan of the revealing of Himself, He said; "Let there be Light"; and there was Light… God called the light Day, and the darkness, He called Night (Evolution). And there was evening and there was morning, a first Day of The Lord. Did you notice the subtlety of the hint in the First Day of The Lord's revealing? Where did darkness come from? You're right neophyte, God revealed Light from what is apparent in the absence of light, darkness covered the face of the deep…

Do not be offended by the word Neophyte, The Minister is only using this word to represent those on whom a new light or way of thinking may be dawning in contrast to the indoctrination of the masses; Neophyte simply describes a person who has been persuaded to change their mental focus concerning their religious faith or other beliefs. (The children of Israel set out on a journey to the promised land. From the moment we are born, I am on a journey from the land of darkness within me to the promised land of Immortality where I will see God within me) ... When the Minister's father was teaching him, and there was a word that the Minister could not understand or did not know, his father would not tell him the meaning but would hand him the dictionary and say,

"**Look it up for yourself!**" Do not accept my understanding of its meaning...

What light? Well, if darkness is eternal, shown by its existence before the spoken creation and light was made known from the darkness, or separated from the darkness, the revealing of the Light can be perceived as the revealing of God's unknown mind. Made known to whom? To those who have been willfully subjected to the illusion of darkness and will seek The Knowledge until the Day of their Salvation has been made complete: "You are my witnesses," declares the Lord, "and my servant whom I have chosen so that you may know and believe me and understand that I am he". Isaiah 43 Remember the long way that the Lord your God has made you travel in the wilderness these forty years, to humble and test you in order to know what was in your heart, whether or not you would keep his commands. He humbled you, causing you to hunger and then feeding you with manna, which neither you nor your ancestors had known, to teach you that man does not live on bread alone (**Matter: modes of vibratory motion**) but on every word that comes from the mouth of the Lord.

Deuteronomy 8

Did you know that a thought hidden in the mind of the thinker is darkness to the world? It is not until the idea is made known by its announcement that then and only then is the idea born but is considered naked for it is just a seed until the conditions for the shedding of the outer shell are present. The conditions must be cultivated by toil or the working of the hands until the seed germinates into life beyond the conditions from which it was formed; thus, making known the brilliance of the perceiving mind in the presence of the darkest darkness light is revealed! The Minister

The 1ˢᵗ Pillar: Liberty, as relates to Man, **Freewill** is the 1ˢᵗ Pillar set up by the Wisdom of God's creation of evolving cycles of Day and Night. All life is regulated by this "Circadian Rhythm". Nothing that is in existence is free or independent from the Law of this cycle. Freewill is governed by this divine law of order. All things created were found to be good according to its purpose. Within its purpose, all things are free (at liberty), Adam is at liberty to live and whatever He perceives as good to put his hands to shall prosper when he is operating within the power and liberty in the Divine Law of Infinite

ADAM Man Convoluted but GOD

Ability. What Law? You are Free to multiply or create as I have created you. As long as Adam is perpetuating righteous life, He is Free. All things are permissible for man but for the Divine Adam, all things are not beneficial according to the purpose of the individual. Harmony with purposeful creation is where our liberty rests. Let us visit the book of Acts to illuminate this principle: A man by the name of Peter will help us understand a little about Law and Liberty. It is said that Peter was commissioned by God to go to Caesarea to witness to Cornelius, a centurion or commander of the army of what was known as the Italian Regiment; to the Jew, the Italians were "Gentiles", the custom of the Jew at that time was that Jews, the "First Born" Child of God could not associate themselves with gentiles. Before we delve deeper, let us come to the same understanding of who a gentile represents in the mind of those viewing themselves as separate and chosen by Yahweh. **Gentile:** one who is not a Jew," c. 1400; earlier "one who is not a Christian, a pagan" (late 14c.), from Late Latin noun use of Latin *gentilis* "of the same family or clan, of or belonging to a Roman gens," from *gens* (genitive *gentis*) "race, clan" (see **genus**, and compare **gentle**). The Latin word then was used in the Vulgate to translate Greek *ethnikos* (see **ethnic**), from *ta ethne* "the nations," which translated Hebrew *ha goyim* "the (non-Jewish) nations" (see **goy**). Hence in Late

Latin, after the Christianization of Rome, *gentilis* also could mean "pagans, heathens," as opposed to Christians. Based on Scripture, *gentile* was also used by Mormons (1847) and Shakers (1857) to refer to those not of their profession.

(http://www.etymonline.com)

As you may have noticed, the word gentile is a word from ancient origin used to denote class, ethnicity, cults, and denominations. To be exact, compared to the Oneness in God, gentile rather than displaying inclusion into the Love of God, implies exclusion from the same based on religious doctrine and ethnicity of the ruling class who portray themselves as worshiping the Creator of all mankind but themselves implement dogma and hatred under the guise religion. Concealed by the euphemism for bigotry: religion is used ever so skillfully to express pious devotion but more often identifies one genre of humans as superior and all others inferior. So, think not that racism is an institution of Satan, for as we can see, those who have this superior view of themselves believe classification of the children was inaugurated by the God of all. Or is that necessarily correct? In the minds of the superior, the inferior serves an inferior god… The story in Acts continues as follows: Cornelius and all his family were devout and God-fearing; he gave generously to those in need and prayed to God regularly. One day at about three in the afternoon he had a vision. He distinctly saw an angel of God, who came to him and said, "Cornelius!" Cornelius stared at him in fear. "What is it, Lord?" he asked.

The angel answered, "Your prayers and gifts to the poor have come up as a memorial offering before God. Now send men to Joppa to bring back a man named Simon who is called Peter, he is staying with Simon the tanner, whose house is by the sea." When the angel who spoke to him had gone, Cornelius called two of his servants and a devout soldier who was one of his attendants. He told them everything that had happened and sent them to Joppa. About noon the following day as they were on their journey and approaching the city, Peter went up on the roof to pray. He became hungry and wanted something to eat, and while the meal was being prepared, he fell into a trance. He saw heaven opened and something like a large sheet being let down to earth by its four corners. It contained all kinds of four-footed animals, as well as reptiles and birds. Then a voice told him, "Get up, Peter. Kill and eat." "Surely not, Lord!" Peter replied. "I have never eaten anything impure or unclean." *(Law of Moses)* The voice spoke to him a second time, "Do not call anything impure that God has made clean." *(Law of Divine Purpose or Grace)* This happened three times, and immediately the sheet was taken back to heaven. While Peter was wondering about the meaning of the vision, the men sent by Cornelius found out where Simon's house was and stopped at the gate. They called out, asking if Simon who was known as Peter was staying there. While Peter was still thinking about the vision, the Spirit said to him, "Simon, three men are looking for you, so get up and go downstairs. Do not hesitate to go with them, for I have sent them." Peter went down and said to the men, "I'm the one you're looking for. Why have you come?" The men replied, "We have come from Cornelius the centurion. He is a righteous and God-fearing man, who is respected by all the Jewish people. A holy angel told him to ask you to come to his house so that he could hear what you have to say." Then Peter invited the men into the house to be his guests.

  Please take note of Divine Purpose and Liberty made manifest in this New Testament story; Peter's body became hungry for physical food, Cornelius and his family were also hungry for food, not physical but spiritual food. God showed Peter that he was free to eat any type of physical food to satisfy his body's need to replenish itself which required communication between matter and spirit (Shaman) to fulfill a lack. Peter recognized the sensation of hunger which ultimately caused him to feed the body but did not readily understand the word of God and would have nullified the Word for the sake of the Law of Moses which was not applicable when involving the Spiritual needs of humanity. Keep in mind as you read, Peter is representing the Jew and Cornelius the gentile. Those who desire to pervert the Law of Liberty, say that Grace according to this passage of text enables believers in Christ to eat those animals which the Law prohibits. Is food the object or subject of this passage? Or is salvation and Freedom in Purpose the main idea with food and Law being but a tool leading the unnatural religious man back to the Oneness of the knowledge of the All in God. To understand the All in God, we first must understand Day as in; "God called the light <u>Day</u>, and the darkness, He called Night. And there was evening and there was morning, a first <u>Day</u>. This day is not a matter of measurement of time, 24 hours as we measure time. God is not concerned with time as is man for God is Eternal. Man, however, has been taught and structured not to reason with the right side of the brain but to be a good citizen of a structured ruling class of left-brain dominant thinkers, where the citizen is told what to think rather than encouraged to exercise reason by association. God was illuminating something when he spoke the world. He was revealing Himself and the first day is the beginning of the 1st stage of man's understanding who God is by His creation, not just understanding God but understanding that God is His Creation, and His Creation is God, these were with God in the beginning...

    For you to accept the identification of a gentile, there had to have been a comparison or the identification of a non-gentile. Since you are a gentile, why does another group of people have to be identified for you to have knowledge of who you are? It is because of what the world has been taught which shows their limited understanding of God. When the question: "Who are you?" is presented, the answer involves the person answering the question to identify themselves in relation to all that is physical, i.e., professions, parents, nationalities etc. This is proof that we are all in all, not one person can be identified physically without the identification of the All. Who are you? You are Not what you have experienced; for what you have experienced has only been created to test what you perceive yourself to be after having contacted illusions of reality Matthew 4:1-11. And what you have become, is a result of who and what you have believed! The ancients were condemned as Sun worshipers because of the frequent reference to the sun, this concluded by the superficial glimpse of their handwritings and symbols on walls and tablets. Were they really sun worshipers, or did they recognize that the sun was like the Son, a representative, ambassador, or essence of God; a consuming fire, unapproachable, giver of light, without whom nothing would exist?

We have learned to describe ourselves as "just a man" or, I am only human, and nobody is perfect. God sees His children as perfect, many who are reading these words have children, how many of you condemn your own children? Why then do we believe God sits eagerly watching, waiting to exercise punishment and calamity upon us with every violation of non-spiritual religious law? Remember that God is Spirit, knows all and the most important essence of Spirit is Immutability, Spirit does not change! Everything was found good for the purpose for which it was created and herein rests the key to our liberty; "Freedom within Purpose". That which God designed to make us free has bound those whose desire is to consume all things, identifying the battle between flesh and spirit. Identifiers set up at the creation of the world were for those who would later be identified as the children of God. The children embrace the boundaries set, for within contains purpose which confounds the wisdom of the children of the world. Whereas the world desires that nothing is off limit, the children of God knows that disobedience limits the freedom of the spirit. What is being said?

We have come to understand that angels are spirit and do not eat or crave the same food that mortal man craves. Therefore, it is not the spirit that is tempted, it is the flesh. The sin that causes eternal spiritual punishment is blasphemy of the

Spirit. The Spirit comes from God who has no darkness in Him, therefore the spirit of man cannot be defiled but by living contrary to righteousness, man lives a lie, bearing false testimony against the spirit who resides within every living being. Therefore, it is said that animals know the righteous requirements of God, but man does not. This is what the world fails to perceive; it is not individual infractions of the law which brings guilt, it is blasphemy – (<u>irreverence</u>, taking the Lord's name in vain, God gave man His Name) which causes Spiritual death is not the same as physical death as all must die for the replenishment of the earth.

Taking the Lord's name in vain? How? We have been created in His image; the word image connotes illusion according to Strong's Thesaurus. Illusion is defined as something that deceives by producing a false or misleading impression of reality, the state or condition of being deceived, misapprehension. God being the Spiritual reality of man, the illusion being that man, as he lives according to the flesh, becomes the false image of God forming the illusion. The purpose of man is to be confronted with the physical by means of his physical senses which produces a world that can be touched, seen etc. as the physical but recognizing that the physical is not the true image of God, just as physical man is not the Spiritual image of God because God is spirit. So then, the entire physical world is but a delusional battlefield to test the righteousness of the word of God: what would the word made flesh do outside of God after having been given its individual physical identity as Adam?

Remember, matter is not solid at all but to the contrary, produced by rapid movement of atoms (or spiritual Adams living on earth), an illusion of solid matter is produced and perceived by the physical senses, illusion because what is seen perverts the unseen. When man sees himself, the illusion is then produced by the fact that he sees himself as flesh rather than Spirit who animates all living matter. (Instead of Christ we see physical Adam) The Spirit who animates all flesh is none other than the Son, yes, the one who the ancients concealed with symbolic writings on stone walls by means of stellar reference (As above so below) the Sun which gives all the living Life. The day of the Lord comes when Adam can take off the garments of flesh and apprehend the Spirit who dwells in them, then the Image of God on earth will be made manifest and all who resides will witness the Glory of the coming of the Lord who was sent to **Make the thing whereto I sent it prosper**, destroying the mindset which created the illusion of life outside of God being life at all. Living in the Day of the Lord means that we can perceive the light in the darkness of matter (To be in harmony with the God principle of creation), recognizing that; *"Nothing rests; everything moves; everything vibrates."*-The Kybalion. Meaning that all is Spirit and Balance. Before we continue along in the spirit, let us be introduced or reacquainted with one of our ancient teachers from whom the word thought originates.

Thoth- was one of the earlier Egyptian gods. He was popular throughout Egypt but was particularly venerated in Khnum (Hermopolis Magna) where he was worshipped as part of the Ogdoad. As the power of his cult grew, the myth was rewritten to make Thoth the creator god. According to this variant, Thoth laid an egg (planted a seed) from which the Egyptian god Ra was born. Other myths suggest that Thoth created himself through the power of language (in an interesting parallel to the phrase in the Gospel according to St John "in the beginning was the word, and the Word was with God, and the Word was God"). The moon and the sun were initially thought of as the left and right eyes of Horus. Although Osiris and Isis were generally credited with bringing civilization to mankind, Thoth was also thought to have invented writing, medicine, magic, and the Egyptian's civil and religious practices. He was even credited with the invention of music, which was more often associated with Hathor. Thoth was the patron of scribes and of the written word. He was scribe of the underworld who recorded the verdict on the deceased in the hall of Ma'at and was given the epithets "He who Balances", "God of the Equilibrium" and "Master of the Balance". Thoth maintained the library of the gods with the help of his wife, Seshat (the goddess of writing). He was the scribe of the gods and was often described as the "*Lord of the Divine Body*", "*Scribe of the Company of the Gods*", the "*voice of Ra*" or the "*counsellor of Ra*" who (along with Ma'at) stood on the sun barge next to Ra on his nightly voyage across the sky. It was also thought that Ra gave Thoth an area of the underworld to rule in the "*Land of the Caves*", He kept a register of those in his realm and decreed just punishments for their transgressions and acted as Ra's representative in the afterlife. In this role, his wife was Ma'at.

It was said that he was the author of the spells in the "*Book of the Dead*" and "*Book of Breathings*" (which was also attributed to Isis) and he was given the grand title, the "*Author of Every Work on Every Branch of Knowledge, Both Human and Divine*". Egyptian mythology speaks of the "*Book of Thoth*" in which the god inscribed all the secrets of the universe. Anyone who read it would become the most powerful sorcerer in the world but would be cursed by their knowledge. Needless to say, people have been searching for this text despite the warning, and some more "*colorful*" theories propose that it is hidden in a secret chamber in or near the Great Pyramid. This book is said by some to be the "*emerald tablets of Thoth*" a work of dubious authenticity. Thoth was a great magician who knew "*all that is hidden under the heavenly vault*". He used his knowledge to help Isis after the murder of her husband Osiris by his brother Set. With the help of Anubis, he created the first mummification ritual and helped resurrect Osiris (albeit in the land of the Dead). He also protected Isis's son Horus by driving a magical poison from his body when he was incredibly young and supported him in his fight to gain the throne which was rightfully his. Many of the Egyptians religious and civil rituals were organized according to a lunar calendar. As Thoth was associated with writing and with the moon it is perhaps unsurprising that he was also linked to the creation of the calendar. As his association with the moon waned, he developed into a god of wisdom, magic, and the measurement of time. Similarly, he was considered to measure and record time. He was known by the epithets; "the One who Made Calculations Concerning the Heavens, the Stars and the Earth", "the Reckoner of Time and of Seasons" and "the one who Measured out the Heavens and Planned the Earth".

Thoth was thought to be the inventor of the 365-day calendar (which replaced the inaccurate 360-day calendar). According to myth, he earned the extra days by gambling with the moon (Iabet or Khonsu) in a game of dice to help the goddess Nut. She was pregnant by her brother / husband Geb, but Ra forbade her to give birth on any day of the Egyptian calendar. Thoth won a portion of light from the moon (1/72) which equated to five new days, and Nut gave birth to her five children on those days (Osiris, Horus the Elder, Set, Isis and Nephthys). He was also known as a good counsellor and persuasive speaker. – **Ancient Egypt Online.**

The Greeks associated Thoth with the messenger god Hermes; Old English *thōht*, of Germanic origin meaning to think. The two deities were combined to form Hermes

Trismegistus (thrice/three times great) and Khmun (An Egyptian god who created human beings from **clay on a potter's wheel**) was renamed Hermopolis (city of Hermes). In the 1670's, the word Hermeneutics was understood as a derivative of Hermes as the divine custodian of speech, writing, and eloquence. **Hermeneutics**: the science of interpretation, especially of the Scriptures, originates from Egyptian myth by way of Greek influence.

The Three Initiates state it best in their book Kybalion in the 9th chapter entitled Vibration- informal a person's emotional state, the atmosphere of a place, or the associations of an object, as communicated to and felt by others. The great Third Hermetic Principle--the Principle of Vibration--embodies the truth that Motion is manifest in everything in the Universe--that nothing is at rest--that everything moves, vibrates, and circles. This Hermetic Principle was recognized by some of the early Greek philosophers who embodied it in their systems. But then, for centuries it was lost sight of by the thinkers outside of the Hermetic ranks. But in the Nineteenth Century physical science re-discovered the truth and the Twentieth Century scientific discoveries have added additional proof of the correctness and truth of this centuries-old Hermetic doctrine.

The Hermetic Teachings are that not only is everything

in constant movement and vibration, but that the "differences" between the various manifestations of the universal power are due entirely to the varying rate and mode of vibrations. Not only this, but that even THE ALL, in itself, manifests a constant vibration of such an infinite degree of intensity and rapid motion that it may be practically considered as at rest, the teachers directing the attention of the students to the fact that even on the physical plane a rapidly moving object (such as a revolving wheel) seems to be at rest. The Teachings are to the effect that Spirit is at one end of the Pole of Vibration, the other Pole being certain extremely gross forms of Matter. Between these two poles are millions upon millions of different rates and modes of vibration.

    Within these millions upon millions of different rates of vibration, mankind bears witness to the power of mind and manifestation; evidence of the power of Spiritual Rest or oneness with the Natural = NTR: Spiritual; Al: of. When natural is referred to in a theological sense, we get our understanding from a pre-Judaism, Kemetic theological understanding of everything it means to Rest on the Sabbath. Not rest on the Sabbath but be in the Sabbath as the Rest of God who operates at such a high rate of vibration that in Him, there is Rest and all exists in His Rest when man exists as his **Natural** self. Man, in his natural state is ordained to continue to "subdue" the earth as found in Genesis 1:28.

This word subdue does not imply having dominion over everything that is eagerly cooperative with man but implies the use of force and intelligence to continue to do God's work on earth and cause earth to be heaven below. The Hebrew word subdue or **kabos** (Mental Substance) denotes a different understanding than that in accepted modern day Christianity which says that man was placed in a garden where death, opposition and enmity were not expected or were a part of natural order. Plants and animals died long before Adam and Eve were sentenced to die for disobedience. It was not disobedience which brought about death, it is the "Religion of the Serpent" which perpetuates disobedience by robbing Adam of his identity as the creative word of God and has caused the God given intelligence to have been replaced by blind faith so that man himself views continuing God's work of civilizing a chaotic world as a curse to have to sweat. Man continues his search for a redeemer while the earth plummets into the pits of an illusionary hell where man will meet **himself**, his only adversary.

Modern Science has proven that all we call Matter and Energy are but "modes of vibratory motion," and some of the more advanced scientists are rapidly moving toward the positions of the occultists who hold that the phenomena of

Mind are likewise modes of vibration or motion. – The Kybalion: The Three Initiates

Some will appreciate the mentioning of Thoth above and some reading this book will not understand why it was included. The title of this chapter is "The Day of The Lord" and some are living prosperously in the light of day but unfortunately, some are perishing in the uncertainties of the night. Why does one seem to prosper and the other seem to fail? **The Power of Thought**, the light in which one lives comes from his ability to process that which comes from without, how you perceive what you are looking at. Your day will not change until you cultivate your land, you are the creator of your culture, you create the medium that cultivates your reality. Thoughts are the substance of things, the day that you are experiencing has been created by you, the mind sitting at the potter's wheel. The story of the Egyptian Thoth is none other than positive thought in action. The Potter's Wheel is the power of mind to transform matter. Thoughts are things literally: Now faith is the substance of things hoped for, the evidence of things not seen. The substance you create is evidence of what you believed. The Words of the author of Hebrews makes it plain: You create what you think about. (Making Brick without Straw in Egypt)

God gave light "to" day and darkness "to" night but

what he did not do is define the day and night for us. He left it up to you and me to determine of what a day consists. A day to one man is 24 hours but another man's day is a lifetime 24 hours being only a moment of his day. The day is not over after the passing of 24 hours, tomorrow has only begun. And what is tomorrow but today when I thought about a better day yesterday. All that was not accomplished yesterday helps to organize your tomorrow! Do you remember when your teacher would make roll call before class would begin? Why did she call each student's name? She wanted to account for everyone in the class, right? Man, you should really learn to be present! She was calling your name to make you accountable, she got your attention and prepared you for what she was getting ready to teach. When the teacher calls your name, we should be Present! Being present in the day is to be Lord of the day! Today is the day you created yesterday when you were responding to a temporary moment. Get it? A moment, a fragment, an illusion, a potter's wheel designed to get you to create your tomorrow. Responding to yesterday, you decide what your tomorrow will be. Yesterday was what it became because you decided what it would be before it ever was. Now that you are present today, your tomorrow will be the day. However, if today you are not present as creator of tomorrow, you will live today again tomorrow, The Lord's Day.

ADAM Man Convoluted but GOD

Now back to those students responding to roll call, some answering present and others answering ""here"" were just that! Some were present and some were just "here" but those who are present left evidence that they were here, we feel their presence!

The enlightening doctrine of the heavenly truth has come to rid the world of the darkness which comes from the obscurity of our Intelligence cleverly obscured by those who would find profit in darkness not light, slavery not Liberty. Liberty to do what? Know God by **being** where He created you, this is your garden, cultivated into being such according to what you can freely believe about God before you were taught about God. *(Those who come, must come as a child)* Freedom of the spirit means that there are not any man-made boundaries set, spirit abides in the law of inheritance. The law of inheritance? Freedom revealed by the releasing of light from the bondage of the unknown says: I must work the works of he who sent me, while it is day: the night cometh, when no man can work. Have you ever really quieted your mind and contemplated, really contemplated beyond all that has been proposed, all that has been suggested, all that has been subliminally infused by religious propaganda and dogma and asked yourself why does modern day man seem so far away from God in comparison to the characters of the Bible who we now view as mighty men and women of God or those who experienced, witnessed, or performed so called miracles? Keep in mind that the majority of those viewed as patriarchs of religious history did not have a <u>book</u> to teach them the requirements and character of God as do, we who are seemingly perishing and spiraling downwardly into the confines of the illumined sarcophagus of dead reason. Reason which says, "God knows my heart", therefore, I am not identified by what I do, and I can do all things because of Grace.

    The Bible did not mysteriously or magically appear from the clouds but has been composed, translated and parts of it rejected and edited by the leaders of the fallen, First Adam's culture. Do we not understand that it was the liberty of those who did not have a book in their presence which enabled the book to be fashioned for those who would ultimately become restricted by the book? What is your inheritance and who defines your God given inheritance?

    On the first day God created… is an indoctrination of religious dogma. The Hebrew rendering of Genesis 1:5 reads: And there was evening and there was morning Yom 1; day 1, 1 day, a first day, but the definitive article "the" in Hebrew is not present and does not initiate a sequence of days but a revealing of God in man who consists of both day and evening;

light and darkness; Spirit and Matter. Adam is all Spirit but without the identifying matter having been made manifest, pure Spirit is God.

Evening: 6150 ereb; eh-reb night. Moses' and the world's Egyptian inheritance has come to enlighten the world but because of the hatred of self, yes, the identifying oneness present in every individual of all ethnicities has been crucified by him who seeks to destroy himself because of his many hues of blackness displayed by the vast colorful variations of mankind. Adam himself has discolored the voice of his own ancestors to propagate a false religion. Can you hear the Minister speaking concerning the Day of The Lord? Evening was craftily used by the spirit to speak to the spirit of those who have ears to hear what the Minister is bearing witness to. Evening means dusk, Adam ate from a tree which caused him to seek a covering that covered his nakedness, not the nakedness of sinful flesh for God did not create sinful man but his thinking became darkened by the very dark matter of his identification as man. There was evening and there was morning, day one is Adam identified as coming into the world, but covered by the flesh, he was not recognized. (God's only begotten Son) **The Neophyte**… Evening: to braid, intermix- (man is a mixture of Dark Matter and Spirit; Light and Darkness) through the idea of covering with a texture; to grow dusky at sundown, to be darkened. See Strong's Concordance.

Darkness was first: representing the absence of the spoken, then came life: the existence of Adam in whom the revelations of God would be known. Day by Day, God is being revealed by what exists, since it is not yet understood what exists (for all matter is subjective substance with infinite potential to be made/transformed), neither is God yet understood. It was through the lens of darkness that Adam recognized himself as fallen and created a doctrine of belief which perpetuates this darkened state requiring the Sacrifice of the innocent for himself to be made free, but then comes morning, the revealing of the age of Resurrection when man will "See In Himself" God. **AMEN-RA!**

ADAM Man Convoluted but GOD

Let Us Make Man In Our Image…

Man, Adam, rmT, Manu, Melchizedek and Mannus. *What is mankind that you are mindful of him, human beings that you care for him? You have made him a little lower than God and crowned him with glory and honor. You made them rulers over the works of your hands; you put everything under their feet: all flocks and herds, and the animals of the wild, the birds in the sky, and the fish in the sea, all that swim the paths of the seas. LORD, our Lord, how majestic is **your name in all the earth!*** (Psalm 8)

Is this a hidden message to the wise from David? Has man been given a name of God to rule the earth? According to this Name of God, does man have the authority to bring all that exists into subjection under One Name? **Majestic:** characterized by or possessing majesty; of lofty dignity or imposing aspect. Does man bring all that exists into subjection? Or does he himself become subjected so that what exists has substance?

The subject of Psalm 8 is Man, the enlightening beauty of this Psalm is that David is not complaining about the fact of man having been made a little lower than God, but to the contrary, he is humbly and fearfully "praising" God. Yes, this is praise for giving man a name that is higher than all others... Let us delve deeper to trouble the waters of mankind's Cognitive identity crisis which causes him to perceive himself through the eyes of the fallen serpent therefore assuming the image of that which he perceived. The word Man also means Adam; ruddy or red like clay can represent individual man or mankind. The Egyptian word for man; rmT represents the original Egyptian man or mankind; the ancient Egyptian viewed himself as the original man. Manu: in the early texts of Hinduism refers to the archetypal man or the same as the modern-day Christian and Jewish thought related to Adam before the fall i.e., progenitor of humanity.

Melchizedek also represents an aspect of man but more specifically, spiritual man who has neither earthly father nor mother. Melchizedek was a Canaanite Priest King whose name means My King is Sedek or to use a euphemism more easily accepted by the religious community; My King is Righteousness. Unacceptable because Sedek also spelled Sydyk was a Canaanite god linked to the planet Jupiter. And now, we get to the name Mannus but before we can expound on this Germanic name representing man, let us first get the history. According to the Roman writer Cornelius Tacitus, Mannus was the son - essence of the god Tuisto believed to have been a god born from the earth. Adam, also born of the earth without earthly mother or father, as is Melchizedek without mother or father, so is Christ without earthly father; please note, the minister is not speaking of the Jesus born of flesh but the Spirit-Man, Christ born of the unseen Father.

Mannus, had three sons according to Germanic mythology just as Adam was the progenitor of three sons, just as Noah, the biblical figure was father of three sons who are representatives of three nations and ethnicities of peoples who spread throughout the earth. This Germanic god Tuisto may have also been known by the name Tiwaz according to his dualistic nature. The diligent student may even be able to perceive resemblance to the god Tammuz worshipped by weeping or mourning for his return due to his effects on harvest (Ishtar, Astarte, and Easter), also known as the god of life-death and rebirth; see Ezekiel 8:14.)

"Then I continued to watch because of the boastful words the horn was speaking. I kept looking until the beast was slain, and its body destroyed and thrown into the blazing fire. (The other beasts had been stripped of their authority but were allowed to live for a period of time.)

"In my vision at night I looked, and there before me was one like a son of man, *(human being)* **The Aramaic phrase bar enash means human being.** *Coming with the clouds of heaven.*

He approached the Ancient of Days and was led into his presence. He was given <u>authority, glory, and sovereign power</u>; all nations and peoples of every language worshiped him. His dominion is an everlasting dominion that will not pass away, and his kingdom is one that will never be destroyed.

"I, Daniel, was troubled in spirit, **{Perplexed by the Image of Man}** *and the visions that passed through my mind disturbed me. I approached one of those standing there and asked him* **the meaning of all this...**

"So, he told me and gave me the interpretation of these things: 'The four great beasts are four kings that will rise from the earth. But the Holy **people** *of the Most-High* **will receive the kingdom** *and will possess it forever—yes, for ever and ever.'*

Then the sovereignty, power, and greatness of all the kingdoms under **heaven will be handed over to the Holy PEOPLE** *of the Most-High.* (Daniel 7)

In case you did not see what I saw in Daniel's vision, let me explain. Daniel saw one man who appeared as the Son of Man, receive authority, glory, and sovereign power. When Daniel asked for an explanation of the things he saw, he was told that the people will receive the kingdom and all power given to the people who were represented by the One Man...

Adam is a traveling Man; Christ is his Infinite Revolution; *activity or movement designed to effect fundamental changes in the socioeconomic situation.* Every human being is Christ, I showed you that every ancient kingdom had its definition or myth concerning man and its original man. Christ is the matter of identity challenged in the garden. It was this spiritual aspect of the man that was in question. Not Jesus the man but man's Lordship on earth. Not to take away from the belief that you may have of a religious savior, but every man is the creator of his own garden for his own thoughts become reality. Every man is set free or imprisoned by his thoughts, he is made or unmade by what he believes and how he perceives all with which he is confronted. Before he enters any situation good or bad, he must first name the circumstance just as Adam named all the animals, man must create his atmosphere. To be clear, he is creator of the conditions by which he will triumph or stumble. Victory to the son because he realizes that he is greater than matter, failure for the man who is defeated in his mind already. Before he physically experiences the event, he first perceives the outcome in his mind, he wins or loses in his own Mental Arena.

If a man commits in his heart, he has already performed with his body. When the term, "son of man" is considered, why do we often think of weakness and sin? Those who have accepted the doctrinal belief of man as weak and suffering, should consider the origin of such a belief. From where does dualistic Adam, divided and at war with himself come? What entity has created the lesser man? How do we justify the forming of two Adams without first considering mental psychosis? The first into which the breath was given, by whose nature was he incomplete? Have you ever really considered what you have been thinking to support this doctrine? Have you thought about your thinking? What is really implied by the idea that before the seed is a seed, it must first be acted upon by a force outside itself before it becomes itself? The very nature of creation makes it clear that in the beginning, there was nothing and from nothing everything existed. Since everything existed, anything that comes after existence, has been created. That which has been created but did not exist in the beginning, must be imagined. Therefore, the lesser Adam creates the conditions by which he is sustained. The unconscious must consider himself as incomplete to survive in his lesser world.

"If he ceases thinking inferior thoughts, his inferior world will be destroyed!"

"When man becomes conscious of the truth, the false disappears."

"When man becomes aware of his wholeness, he will lack nothing."

Then and only then will the earth yield its fruit to that Man, for that man does not speak from lack but he knows all that exists. He who possess the divine Gift of God, speaks as if it has been done already, for **he remembers his future** into the Present… He dwells in that which he perceives for himself…

We are no longer waiting on the Holy Ghost to come but God has set up every situation in your life and is waiting on you to bring the Holy Ghost face to face with your situation.

Furthermore, since what we know of creation makes it clear that Adam was formed from a complete thought, in fact, a righteous thought gave life to him through thought uttered. When a thought is considered and contemplated in the mind, it is sacred at the least because it is unknown except to the mind of the one who thinks it. What causes a man to perceive of himself in any other light than the conceived image formed in mind of the one who created him? His perception of himself is then learned behavior for just as before he was born, he was unknown to the world, {*in this unknown state, the self was Holy*} once born, the world around him reveals him to himself, who he knows is not himself, he has been made in the image of those living in the world around him. Those living in the world, did not create the world but the infant Adam receives his impression of the world from them. The man he becomes, is not the Spirit he was in the beginning, for those living in the world crucified him. By the time this creation, "son of man" is between the ages of 35 and 40, his true self unknown, Life sends him into exile, {*beginning of a crisis*} to find himself.

The first man made known by the world dedicates most of his energy and time to his limitations rather than to his liberty, he believes he is cursed. Cursed because he must work to create his own favorable conditions… Cursed because the world created, he must form… Cursed because **life is in the toil…** God gave life; man contemplates death. God gave freedom of spirit; man perceives the limitations of the flesh. God said greater are the things unseen; man says, if I cannot see it, I cannot use it. The Lord God formed the man out of the **dust;** pulverized from the ground and breathed the breath of life into his nostrils…

{*Like air into a hollow organ, the Ghost/mystery of man was infused*} "but the man is still waiting on someone else, He knows not Himself"…

The man became a living being when life was blown into him; but the man who desires food for the flesh, dies when he finds himself. The man whom God gave dominion over His kingdom became subject to the conditions of the temporary. Desiring life that he could touch with his hand and taste with his mouth, he wanted to see but was blinded by the tree in the center of the garden. He said the serpent is wise and he is living in that tree. The serpent is graceful and full of life, and he is eating the fruit thereof. Let me touch it and eat the fruit thereof and I too may be full of life and graceful, let me reason with the way of the serpent to learn its wisdom so that I may make myself like someone else.

Within the man is his Conscious Self and Subconscious Self

Naked he comes into the world, by what he reasons, he is made known. I have seen many who have reasoned falsely in a world of duality, who he believes himself to be is exactly who the world sees but who he has presented to the world is not who he wants to be. So, Adam is divided, a conscious being because what he sees he believes and subconscious because in him, a man speaks to him. That man is invisible to the world, but the world sees his emotion. Emotion being the life of the inner man pressing outward causing his countenance to express dissonance. No wonder he does not smile. It is the attainment of those things outside of himself, perceived by the senses which obscures man's knowledge of himself and hinders his attainment of spiritual awareness, be it fear, love, money, emotional pain, or gratification. These powerful forces are at work in him, shaping, forming, discomposing him. These building blocks of his personality become him, day after day, thought after thought, experience upon experience, he forges his reality.

The true wickedness then becomes a "false reality" a fortress set up in the mind of man causing him to love a life which does not exist and to become a man who never really knew life. Spiritual wickedness in high places, takes new meaning. especially when thought is solidified by presentation. Presentation being a man's thoughts becoming matter. That which matters to the man, he responds… He keeps being confronted with himself until he becomes… The condition of the world is his formed matter.

What does it mean to fall? The answer to this question is the nucleus of our modern day thought of ourselves and the nature of man. The online dictionary defines the word fall in these terms: *to drop or descend under the force of gravity, as to a lower place through loss or lack of support.* This is the definition used to describe a fall involving the natural body which is affected by the orderly force known as gravity. This gravity is basically the effects which space and time have on matter, the shaping of our physical selves according to science, is due to the unseen force of the universe. Science recognizes this force as universe, theology here identifies God as this same force. Although there seems to be an argument concerning the theory of relativity, we are speaking one and the same language concerning the physical body but not so for the Spiritual man who transcends the physical plane and thus identifies the fallacious fall with its origin occurring in the mind of man.

Since what Adam ate is a matter affecting the life he experienced, then a contrast of food selections naturally occurs. The foods that a hungry man will eat when there are unlimited options and choices available to him are different from the man who longs for food when he is starving and malnourished and his options are few. The latter man develops a different palate motivated from the lack of satisfying substance. When the unconscious soul creates while perceiving lack, the manifestation of his desire must reflect lack and all who learns from him also eats from his source. Everything he creates everything that comes forth from him reflects the source. {*The center of his garden*} That which is central in him produces life; because of his thoughts, he perceived nakedness although he was fully dressed. On this natural plane, gravity is the force that gives objects its shape. In the spiritual, there is also an unseen force by which matter is molded and becomes known by its garments. Those who are given the faculty of reason perceive this transformation from the unseen to the seen as a fall. Parents who have been raised on a particular diet have conceived children and shared with them their DNA.

{DNA or Do Not Accept} To share one's parent's

DNA suggests that the conscious child raised on the same self-restricting and self-limiting diet will develop the same physical ailments as one or both parents. Food, forbidden fruit then remains in the center of the Garden. In the center of the garden is where the DNA exchange takes place, and here in the garden, the subconscious man comes to life. The fall is not then congenital as if from birth but congenital by learned repetitious behavior. (If I continue that thought, I will take you too deep and some of you are not yet ready to walk on water). The fallen mentality states that we were once existing at a certain status and now because of the physical body, we are no longer eternal. Let me explain by beginning with the sacrifice and offering of Cain and Abel. These brothers who once existed as DNA inside Adam and Eve's reproductive organs, represent the spirit and flesh. The two never offered a sacrifice but to the contrary presented habitual behaviors as representation of their eternal lives. The life they lived, presented as offerings. How were their lives an offering to God? What did their lives offer to man? Their story identifies and supports the idea of man's identity crisis and his creation of a world and knowledge derived from lack.

What does Cain and Abel identify except for the seed from which they blossomed? These brothers identify the condition of Adam's mind and what modern man is creating and has created here on earth today. Man substantiates the physical while suppressing the power of spirit and because of this thinking, man is Cain drifting as a lonely wanderer on earth powered by spiritual lack. Abel has been murdered so I am but an empty vessel spreading a doctrine of death and sacrifice for the dead. But who has believed our message and to whom has the arm of the Lord been revealed? For what they were not told, they will see, and what they have not heard, they will understand. Man has been trapped in the world and mind of Adam; physical man craving physical food, unaware of the power of thought, the religious man, fallen man desires a miracle in the form of manna, that which he does not have to perceive. He does not comprehend the power of thought manipulating matter, he blames his parents for his disease.

God, why did you allow me to get involved in the toils of this world which have caused much grief? If only you would have stopped me, I would be better off, I would not have had so many painful life experiences, causing so much regret. How could a loving and merciful God allow for so much trouble in my life? Many have had this thought when faced with the consequence of ill-informed decisions.

"Life is not hard, the hard part about life is living with the decisions we make."

Most of our perceived trouble comes from being

unable to get what we want when we want it! But, let me explain so that we may travel the road of revelation together and find a common destination of truth. Man has a conscious and subconscious mind. Ideally, the subconscious should be more effective at creating and bringing forth fruit in one's life, but most are driven by the conscious mind and only obtain what is visible in their minuscule bubble of reality. Although the subconscious mind is a servant of the conscious, the subconscious mind is greater, greater because it, The Subconscious Mind is ruler of the universe. Minister, what does this have to do with food for the body? Be careful what you crave because all that we blame God for, we have called into our own lives by thought. Not just any and random thought but focus and precision have caused this bountiful harvest of pain. What you have meditated on, has been given you. What else is prayer if it is not intentional and deliberate thought? It is believed that prayer is but reciting memorized lines and verses of scripture to remind God of His word and telling Him our problems, thanking Him for delivering us from such problems etc. Christ's disciples fell asleep during his prayers, why? He went into meditation, yes meditation! Prayer is meditation, what you dwell and focus on with a precise and deliberate mind is what is made manifest in your life.

When you sit on your couch, when you get on the

phone and talk about problems and lack, when you lie down at night and think about, when you name your troubles by name, you are meditating on and praying for Problems to persist in your life! Food for the body: it is simple; Let us use some text from the Bible to explain this point, if you have raced with men on foot and they have worn you out, how can you compete with horses? If you cannot understand the physical, the physical being conditions as instruments to elevate your thinking, how can you desire to live as a spiritual being?

Melchizedek was Priest of Salem in Canaan; God told the then "pagan" Abram to go to Canaan. The land Canaan is a physical dwelling just as Egypt is physical but represents a place of spiritual awakening and resurrection. Canaan represents a state in the traveler's life where he is crucified, buried, and raised from the dead, a new creature. Christ had to partake of the same transformation, he had to Become someone else, take off his divine garments so that he could be recognized by the physical eye. On earth, in a physical form, he mastered his subconscious thought. The womb from which he came did not define his DNA, his refusal to allow his environment to interfere with his destiny, identified his eternity…

The interesting similarity here between the man we call Adam, the entity we call Self and the Savior we call Christ is the fact that they originated in the same Garden. The earth, the physical dwelling where man who is either elevated or destroyed by how he perceives and manipulates darkness. Is darkness continuing to trouble you or are you starting to rejoice because you want more of this manna? Your land of Canaan is the physical developer of the mysterious Melchizedek. Do not get lost because the Minister is bringing to climax the title of this chapter: Let Us Make Man In Our Image. You have been developed by the physical food that you have planted in your garden. He prepares a table for me in the presence of mine "enemies" (take away enemy and replace with enigma to = mine enigma) when you finally understand this, you will have understood the enemy never existed outside of you. The dark son of Ham represents our physical darkness in which exists the light of the world. Melchizedek represents the physical man after having come out of the fire no longer living as a physical man for all flesh was consumed by the fire...

(Those long dark nights have taught you to see the light which exists in darkness; your spiritual self has been born from darkness; out of Egypt, I called my Son).

This spiritual man Melchizedek, Adam, Mannus and Egyptian rmT is he who has been sent into destiny and is now Priest of the perceived dark world, perceived; for these were only illusions and shadows... You created them; God did not have anything to do with it! You should now be gradually understanding why the word Adam is ambiguous in its meaning: physical man, mankind or simply a man named Adam. You were created a spiritual being. For however many years you have been in your body, you have been weaving the garments which you now wear. The physical garments encompassing the senses and all that makes man a living being on earth, veils the eternal identity of man. The eternal man once released by the vicissitudes of life is The Priest of the New Salem. As Priest, you are the unseen power and knowledge of God; the Arm of Isaiah 53:7, the force and gravitational effect which causes change on earth. Once you realize that you have the same power of attraction to call forth every good thing into your life just as gravity calls forth all matter to earth, then you will live as leader, the head and not the tail.

Christ stirred up a mass following, affecting change everywhere he went. Gravity pulls matter towards the center of the earth, when God is your center and your agenda is righteousness, all men are drawn to WHO? Yes… He is in you.

You are "He" whom the power of God has been given to bring all that exists into subjection under One Name. You are His gravity attracting life to the God in you who shapes and forms the sustaining foundation of the mansion being built for your dwelling place. In heaven? Yes, heaven is now your new home because you dwell where earthly men cannot comprehend. You are the Mansion; you are the house of God. Stop facing life as a mortal, stop creating from the blueprint of lack! The intelligent modern man have become exhausted because of the wisdom of ancient man and are attempting to understand the marvelous structures erected by those who predated modern intelligence by thousands of years. The question is asked, "How could they who had no vehicle to travel into outer space know how to construct these earthly structures in line with objects of the cosmos. The ancients used the same vehicle that is available to both you and I; Know Thy Self… AND THE HEAVENS WILL NO LONGER BE A MYSTERY TO YOU.

    These things revealed by the spirit have always been present before our eyes but a veil of darkness we have been blinded by… The word universe for example, has been attempting to reveal the true essence of man to the world but religious dogma has told the man that nothing good comes from him; let us see for ourselves. Uni = one, verse = turned – Latin – universus: combined into one whole. Individually, man is one, it is only when they agree to come together will God be made manifest (Master Mind). The universe is the manifestation of God. Haven't you heard that we are all going back to God? The term: "Back to God" itself is evidence of Adam's cognitive dissonance for we even now, remain in the mind of God. Remember that God returned to the place in the Garden where He would talk to the man and woman (Subconscious Mind), but the man hid himself, to hide was man's delusional behavior and sinful desire, not willing to be subject to the Creator. Darkness implies being away from God, out of His mind. He it is that is truly out of his mind is he who believes himself to exist outside the mind of God. Consider this question for clarity; What does it mean to be conscious? To be conscious, is for one to be awake and aware of one's surroundings. To be conscious, one must first be aware. If he does not know the quintessential substance of that place where he dwells, that man cannot possibly reach out and take from the prosperity of the land (Tree of Life).

We can say with confidence then that Adam was at first conscious, for he talked with God. With his hand, he could grasp what his conscious mind could see. His hand could not handle what his mind did not first perceive, and neither could he live in a place where he did not believe. Adam in the Garden, is the "Conscious Man", reaping the harvest of his own thoughts... The idea of a dark world outside of the Garden, waiting for resurrection is an imagined myth of Man and his religion. Ask yourself "Since God created the Garden and placed the man therein, who created the world that is Outside of Paradise? Man creates his world and lives in it... It is only when man can fully comprehend the words of the Moses of modern times when he said in his I have a dream speech. *"I have a dream that one day, down in Alabama, with its vicious racists, with its governor having his lips dripping with the words of "interposition" and "nullification" -- one day right there in Alabama little black boys and black girls will be able to join hands with little white boys and white girls as sisters and brothers. I have a dream today!"*

I have a dream that one day every valley shall be exalted, and every hill and mountain shall be made low, the rough places will be made plain, and the crooked places will be made straight", it is the end of this statement by Martin Luther King that is most proverbial: and the **glory of the Lord shall be revealed, and all flesh shall see it together."** All flesh will see God and His son will no longer live in the dark recesses of his own mind… I and my father are One Mind!

Cognitive Dissonance & Superstitious Ideology...

Cognitive Dissonance: the state of having inconsistent thoughts, beliefs, or attitudes, especially as relating to behavioral decisions and attitude change.

In the field of psychology, **cognitive dissonance** is the mental discomfort (psychological stress) experienced by a person who simultaneously holds two or more contradictory beliefs, ideas, or values.
(https://en.wikipedia.org/wiki/Cognitive_dissonance)
We have all seen at least once the statue of the man sitting on a stoop with his elbow on his leg and chin on fist, "Thinking Man" posture. Looking at that figure, it is natural to form the conclusion: He is in deep thought. What if we were to assume that this now statue was once a living person turned into stone by nature of what he contemplated. In other words, we, and the environment in which we live are either transformed by our thoughts or are paralyzed by the same! A man's thoughts may paralyze him or liberate him. Move him or hold him captive, turn him into an unproductive object of ridicule or cause him

to be the image of a god. Because we hold a thought in our minds, does not indicate that we have used the thinking process to analyze the thought. Take for example the following: *Man perceives God as Holy and Divine but as for the image that God casts upon the earth, the same man perceives as wicked.*

When the above thought is analyzed or unpacked, we are forced to consider the concept or the very idea of the thought not as a whole but analyzing each word. To see a man with a suitcase simply gives the idea of travel but unpacking and analyzing the contents may lead to determining his destination. Man perceives God – Man (Homo sapiens) wise or rational man, finite man perceives infinite God. For rationalization to take place, or a comparison to be made, there must be a prototype against which to compare. To whom or what can the infinite be compared, where is the prototype? He must be found within what has been created, he must be found on earth. The closest and most rational prototype could only be man for man alone can perceive this thought or conceptualize the concept of the infinite! Therefore, since man gets angry, his god which he forms also gets frustrated by things he cannot understand and is afraid of things he cannot know, the building blocks of anger. For whom else should we compare the creator? "Let Us Make Him" like us, for concerning man according to Shakespeare, *"What a piece of work* is man! How noble in reason! How infinite in faculties! In form and moving how express and admirable! In action how like an angel! **In apprehension how like a god.**

When I observe Your heavens, the work of Your fingers, the moon, and the stars, which You set in place, what is man that You remember him, the son of man that You look after him? You made him little less than God and crowned him with glory and honor. You made him lord over the works of Your hands; You put everything under his feet: all the sheep and oxen, as well as the animals in the wild, the birds of the sky, and the fish of the sea that pass through the currents of the seas. **Yahweh, our Lord, how magnificent is Your name throughout the earth!** Psalm 8 HCSB.

What has inoculated God's Adam? What has pierced his soul? Why is Adam experiencing the psychological stress of an individual who simultaneously holds two or more contradictory beliefs concerning the nature of God? The way man reacts to his fellow man is evidence of his lack of understanding of God's nature not of his own. Evil comes not to question God's man but to cause man to convey false testimony about his Man's God. Every man is different and not one man represents the image of God without that man realizing that God made one man, the Son of All Man in the image of himself. Here is a concept beyond man's understanding: The Son of Man or the Son who lives in man. What is the image that God gave every man?

Image: "copy, imitation, likeness; statue, picture," also "phantom, *ghost*." In the likeness of God, He did create them. The word likeness derives from the Old English word gelic which conveys the sense of wonderfully pure, sweet. In God's wonderfully pure state, He created man. In the guise of man, God walked the earth, but darkness would not allow Him to be fully known. When the sound of God was heard during the breeze of the evening, man hid his true nature for he no longer recognized himself. For he now rejects the very Ghost of God. This is the Cognitive Dissonance of man; his Ghost haunts him. This began long ago with superstitious ideology.

    We should start this chapter by understanding the message of the Babylonian Tower of Babel. Sons and daughters (the very Essence of God) were scattered to the four corners of the earth so that Love could conquer all who call themselves children of God. Love in this sense is the Love that allows us to stop looking "at" a man and start seeing the man. Attempting to find God, a tower was built, attempting to know God we must perceive the whole man, the substance of his being. Not just the outer substance but the inner. God cannot be known by looking at man, but God may be revealed by seeing the man! Unless the stuff which makes up the man is known, God is hidden. The contents of the man, the stuff that gives him character causes those without love to abandon him, he is a sinner! No, out of darkness the light has revealed the darkness in you for you have rejected the call to Love... For the very substance, the stuff of man is God. A man with a suitcase reveals that he may be a traveler, but his origin and destination remain a mystery until the bags he carries are unpacked. It takes Love to unpack a man's suitcase... Let us begin to unpack the man's suitcase and reveal his garment.

Adam has been sent a powerful delusion to perceive that which does not exist. If Satan is a lie and the father of lies, who was the first to mention this lie? God did not mention the Serpent, why is it that man revealed the serpent to God? Every man's deed is the revealer of his own thoughts. The word serpent means to be known of its hiss, the sound it makes, its character and its deeds. The man's works outside the Mind of God is the Serpent, yes that ancient dragon who breathes fire against God and the sons of God against whom the serpent makes war here on earth willed from heaven for his own thoughts. Search every religion, and you will find man as the enforcer of its bylaws and doctrine. Search every religion and you will find a murderer who believes that he must kill to keep his religion safe. The first religion given to man was given by the mind of the serpent who gave the man false religious beliefs as the word of God and Adam believed it, therefore creating death as a result of departure from God's mind. Man's only means of survival in his new world was to create for himself doctrines and ideologies perpetuating the religion of darkness as his light. *"Because they did not love the truth… For this reason, God sends them a powerful delusion, so they will believe the lie."*

    The serpent could not talk but it does make a sound. (Then the man and his wife heard the sound of the Lord God walking in the garden) Gen. 3:8 They did not see but heard or perceived the Spirit of God. Does the Book say they saw God? Does the Book say she saw the serpent? Hebrew word for serpent means according to its hiss: (The power of suggestion) The serpent can only hiss or psst. As if to get your attention or divert your attention away. Satan has no power except for that which those who have the authority give him: authorize or allow. Being that the serpent could not talk, man gives word and life to the serpent according to his own desire so that it is not the serpent who is outside of the man but the man who has taken or have become his image; consuming; becoming mesmerized by the way of the serpent. Freewill given to man to freely seek and serve God thus in the beginning a worshipping angel Lucifer after which Satan. But what is it that caused the fall? Who is the serpent? God given position and freedom of man. The serpent is freedom the tree represents principle (Tree of the knowledge of good and evil) after the consumption represents perversion of the freedom of man. Come let us reason together; all men are rational beings, able to learn by means of what he puts his hands to, simply put; by what he experiences; upon what his eyes focus, and his experiences are the realities of what he can perceive. (2 Thessalonians 11)

To make this plain, when it comes to the symbol of the serpent, for since the beginning, man has been aware of the voice of God. Not an external voice but an inner voice which comes from the belly, the visceral of man. We grow in the natural to understand the voice of our parents and a stranger we will not follow unless we have not become fully grown. Then, the man can think, or the man has a mind to think and what he thinks is conditioned by his environment. How many of us have desired a thing and was sure that God had satisfied us with the object of our desire only to find out that it was not God who said yes but our free will to rationalize a desired end or answer. When we are sure enough because of reason, it is typical to say, "God said", but when that which we believed turns into grief, we see clearly and relieve God from blame and suggest, "God could not have told me to do the thing that failed but instead the "serpent" for self would not injure self". Rather than perceiving growth through the experience of failure, man who perceives and now has the knowledge of good and evil believes that Adam cast out of the garden is death and not growth, let us not forget that man does not die, the spirit only transitions. It is through the imagination that the man can perceive himself out of his natural or physical environment.

Whatever the reality, it can be distorted by the mind be it a carnal mind or spiritual for man has the authority to walk in heaven but live-in hell. Adam's thinking caused his dwelling to change, he could not continue to possess heaven with an earth-bound mind. The way in which a man thinks, so shall his environment be. Change the mind and the address will change. The environment of the man sustains him and gives him life, death sets him free when his mind expands beyond the fruits of the field "Tree". It is safe to say that because the man was willing to grow, he imagined the serpent never mentioned by God but from the imagination of the man did Leviathan become a reality! The mind of man can cause that which does not exist to suddenly Be. Who else has the power to say let it Be and it was except for the Son? Who else can say to this mountain go throw yourself into the ocean except for the one lead by the Spirit of God? Or who can say, "Let Us Make Man Conform To Our Image"? In Romans 1:22 Paul states:
Claiming to be wise, they became fools and exchanged the glory of the

immortal God for images resembling mortal man, birds, four-footed animals, and reptiles, snakes, dragons, and The Serpent that the man put in the Tree. Tree? Yes "Tree" as meant by definition: a woody perennial plant, typically having **a single stem or trunk growing to a considerable height and bearing lateral branches at some distance from the ground.**

In other words, Tree – take a tree like form which starts from a single seed or singleness of thought, a focused mind can create, bring to being all things that he believes. This is called disciplined or deliberate thought, which is described as a "single eye" or seed as in tree that exists but is not yet seen only the seed but has always existed but not yet made known only but a "shell" of that which was to come, The Tree is the principle, not the serpent. Before the serpent was mentioned, death was the reward for mishandling of the Tree, the Principle. Ask yourself, what is the reason of your grief? You have been mishandling the Principle upon which creation rests: there cannot be success without obedience to the Law! - Perennial Tree! (Perennial= lasting or existing for a long or apparently infinite time; enduring or continually recurring. For those who understand; an **Evergreen**) The ideas of the man are its lateral branches extending or affecting everything within its shade. Just as Adam sinned, they all partook of the Tree for they believed the Ideas of Man!

The Fall of Man Genesis 3:1-19

In the garden where all that has been created is announced as good, there exists a life that is contradictory to the source of its own existence, God created heaven and earth, man and the wise serpent caused the earth to become void and formless. The book of Genesis begins with the voice of God manifesting life, chapter two details the life that exists in His Logos. Chapter three begins with the iconography of the Serpent who is revealed by the Logos as an animal which becomes the symbol of wickedness and death, instrumental in the fall of man, necessitating the incarnate Christ. In fact, chapter 3 begins with three words as its introduction, "Now the serpent", introducing not man as the subject of this chapter but an animal that is able to communicate with man. Not simply casual communication but possessing the power of persuasive logos which appeals to the reason of the man created in God's image. Not only does this serpent display this persuasive logos during interaction with man but also with an interaction with God himself in Job 2:3 where it is written, "Even though you incited Me against him."

This serpent did not as one commentator comments "cause God" but proposed to God with the same anthropomorphic tongue[14] used in proposing the question to the woman, "Did God really say?" From where and whose mind is the origin of this ophidian symbology? Was this negative stigma attached to the serpent because of its deceitful speech in the garden? Or could it have possibly been because of its characteristics and habitat outside of the garden in the minds and cultures of those of the ANE. From man's experiences on earth with created things comes the formation of his ideas and imaginations concerning those things which he only knows from association. This type of gained or empirical knowledge can be expressed as man's informed imagination. It is from the imagination of man that everything created by man exists. Nothing that has been created by man exists without first having been held in the mind of the man. To be exact, God destroyed the world as written in Genesis 6:5 because of the evil imagination of man. The author of Genesis was himself familiar with serpent iconography through his Egyptian culture. It is quite common to see on the crowns or heads of Egyptian Pharaohs and kings, the image of a snake or cobra. This depiction of royal power dates to before the Predynastic Period of 3100 B.C. representing the Egyptian goddess Wedjat implying the self-renewing power of the

---

[14] Franz Delitzsch, *Biblical Commentary on the Book of Job*, vol. 1, *(Classic Reprint)* (Norwood, Mass.: Forgotten Books, 2012),67.

divinity.[15] W. Foerster a known German philosopher contributed to the 1964 version of the Theological Dictionary of the New Testament, commenting on the serpent he wrote,

"Of all the beasts, the serpent was regarded as demonic in antiquity, thereby revealing the duality of the ancient conception of demons. It plays a great part in Persian, Babylonian, Assyrian, Egyptian and Greek mythology and in essence, this role is always the same; it is a power of chaos which opposed God either in the beginning or at the end of things, or both."[16]

CONTEXT

Genesis 3:1-19 is written by Moses, the Law giver and founder of Israel's faith who became the spiritual leader of a people who were slaves in the land of Egypt. When Moses near the age of 40 according to Acts 7:23, decided to visit his fellow Israelites, he witnessed the beating of one of them by an Egyptian which sparked a turn of events leading to the worship of Yahweh. The Bible uses a specific phrase in describing what had to have taken place before Moses was able to witness the

---

[15] Anne Baring and Jules Cashford, *The Myth of the Goddess: Evolution of an Image* (New York, N.Y.: Penguin, 1993),236.

[16] Gerhard Kittd, *Theological Dictionary of the New Testament (Volume III)* (Grand Rapids, MI: William B. Eerdmans Publishing Company, 1964),281.

beating of the Israelite slave. He could not witness and be moved with compassion concerning that which he had no knowledge of or relationship with. In Pharaoh's house, Moses had a relationship with the Egyptians as Pharaoh's heir. Exodus 2:11 makes it clear that Moses had to "go out" to witness, by specifically stating, "he went out unto his brethren, and looked on their burdens." KJV. Before he could become the founder of faith in Yahweh, Moses had to first come out, and only then could he look or perceive intimately their burdens. This student is highlighting the point above to establish the historicity of Moses' psyche which influenced the contents of Genesis 3:1-19 which begins with the preparatory word now. Now is defined as; used with the sense of present time weakened or lost to introduce an important point or indicate a transition; as of ideas.[17] Moses uses the word now as a discourse marker drawing attention to the introduction of the serpent.

The serpent has a pivotal role in the shaping of man's future on earth and is significant in the minds of the ANE representing evil and a symbol of healing and wisdom in the minds of those who witnessed the effects of its deadly venom, and its shrewd and crafty ways portraying wisdom to lure its

---

[17]Merriam-Webster, *The Merriam-Webster dictionary.*, Home ed. (Springfield, Mass.: Merriam Webster, 1998),356.

prey. To gain a proper understanding of this transition to the serpent and the fall of man, we must consider ancient texts of Moses' surroundings. Longman and Dillard states, "The creation account should be studied in the context of ancient Near Eastern, especially and in particular Babylonian and Ugaritic texts."[18] These authors consider several such ANE creation texts. It is critical for us to consider the topic of good and evil and the concept of chaos or an enemy or opposition to righteousness. Not just in opposition to righteousness but chaos as mentioned by Longman and Dillard, takes the form of a sea monster named Tiamat who is against Marduk the god of the Babylonians.[19] We see the battle of good and evil again in the Ugaritic myth of Baal and the sea god Yam. In Genesis 1:2, the darkness upon the face of the deep resembles the above myths when it is considered that the Spirit of God moved upon the waters then comes creation.

"The definition of a word is going to be directly related to the culture in which that word is being used. One word may have different meanings depending on the culture that is using

---

[18] Tremper Longman and III & Raymond B. Dillard, *An Introduction to the Old Testament*, 2nd ed. (Grand Rapids, Mich.: Zondervan, 2006),52.

[19] Tremper Longman and III & Raymond B. Dillard, *An Introduction to the Old Testament*, 2nd ed. (Grand Rapids, Mich.: Zondervan, 2006),52.

it. To use in proper context a Hebrew word from the ancient Hebrew language, one must first understand Ancient Hebrew thought."[20]

Benner goes on to state that there is a difference between Greek abstract thought and Hebrew concrete thought. Concrete thought expresses concepts and ideas in ways that can be seen, touched, smelled, tasted, and touched. With this understanding in mind, it would not require a stretch of reason to acknowledge the iconography of the serpent used by Moses in expressing man's evil inclination to those like-minded Israelites who were grumbling along the journey from Egypt to the promised land and who were subject to discipline and judgement by Yahweh for their own evil inclinations as evidenced in those who would not enter God's rest. This view is supported by commentators of the Stone Edition Chumash who writes, "The consensus of the commentators is that the serpent of the narrative was literally a serpent. They differ regarding what force it represented: The Evil Inclination, Satan or the Angel of Death."[21] Moses seems to take up the cause of

---

[20] Jeff A. Benner, *The Ancient Hebrew Lexicon of the Bible: Hebrew Letters, Words and Roots Defined Within Their Ancient Cultural Context* (College Station, TX: Virtualbookworm.com Publishing, 2005),11.

[21] with a commentary anthologized from the rabbinic writings by Nosson Scherman, *The Chumash: The Torah, Haftaros and Five*

the condition of man by stating, "now the serpent" to those who had knowledge of the fiery serpents of Numbers 21:6-9 that God sent to destroy those who spoke against Him in the desert.

CONTENT

During the conversation between the woman and the serpent, it does not appear that the woman is surprised that an animal speaks or communicates with those made in the image of God nor that the being with whom she was speaking was evil. Instead, she intertwined and participated in a discussion with a snake concerning a conversation of which the serpent was not privy according to the absence of biblical documentation pertaining to the serpent's presence during the interaction between man and God. The only reasonable dwelling for the serpent during the conversation between the Adam and God would be that the Serpentine Inclination dwelled in Adam where also is his own desire.

Where was the woman's husband and covering during this conversation with the serpent? Hensley states, "Adam stood idly by, abdicating his divinely given responsibility to

---

Megillos = [ḥamishah Ḥumshe Torah, 11th ed. (Brooklyn, N.Y.: Mesorah Pubns Ltd, 2000),15.

guard the garden."[22] What is interesting from the passage though is that the serpent who was not mentioned at the time the command not to eat from the tree of the knowledge of good and evil was given to man, knew the command. The author tells the story with the expectation that the reader should know that the serpent could rationally and intelligently speak to a human. Not only could he speak but while God who is Spirit is speaking with Adam could come in and hear God's personal conversation with Adam and then interpret it in such a way as to deceive the woman. The author of Genesis 3 does not state that God knew that a malevolent spirit was lurking in the Garden He created or that this malevolent spirit had access to a Garden that God could lock and protect as seen when God cast the man and woman out. Furthermore, Adam who was at this time without the knowledge good and evil neither does the bible make mention of Adam's awareness of the existence of such a powerful spirit that could rival God and influence man. It can also be said here that Adam had no fear of death because he had no such knowledge of it as Eugene H. Merrill states, "One must conclude that animals, as part of that

---

[22] Adam D. Hensley, "Redressing the Serpent's Cunning A Closer Look at Genesis 3:1" The ATLAS collection, the American Theological Library Association. Logia, 27 no 3 Holy Trinity 2018, p 41-44.

creation, became subject to death at the same time as man."[23]

The woman was not speaking to a physical snake verbally, but as is written in the Jewish Chumash, the serpent did indeed represent the woman's innate evil inclination represented by the serpent who spoke to her through its presence on and association with the tree as its habitat. It was the wisdom of the serpent, his characteristics and traits which spoke to the woman's imagination and enticed her to eat. What is understood by this student is that the account of Genesis documented in the bible was not the only creation story of the ANE. Mesopotamia has its story of the beginnings; Egypt has its story of the beginnings and so does the Babylonians, documented in the Enuma Elish.[24] The people who were familiar with the beliefs and traditions concerning this mysterious animal did not need an explanation from Moses to understand what the serpent represented in their, and the culture of the ANE as explained in the Archeological Study Bible in its commentary on The Serpent Motif in Other Ancient Near Eastern Literature. "Throughout most of the

---

[23] Eugene H. Merrill, "Pre-Human Death and the Effect of the Fall" The ATLAS collection, the American Theological Library Association. era ns.14/1 (Fall 2016) 15-22.

[24] Tremper Longman and III & Raymond B. Dillard, *An Introduction to the Old Testament*, 2nd ed. (Grand Rapids, Mich.: Zondervan, 2006),52.

ancient Near East, people revered and often worshiped serpents as symbols of royalty, wisdom, healing, fertility, death and other forces, both harmful and beneficent."[25]

There should be no surprise to the modern reader to see the Israelites of Hezekiah's day worshiping the Nehushtan in 2 Kings 18:4. The serpent as a symbol of antithesis to God and adversary of man did not originate with Moses and the writing of Genesis but existed long before Moses' day as is also mentioned by Bruce Waltke describing how the writer of Genesis would have used ANE stories. He writes, "Inspired by the Holy Spirit, the biblical authors stripped the ancient pagan literatures of their mythological elements." As can be seen by this statement, Waltke acknowledges the use of pagan literature however transformed the literature may be, the stories have its origin in other than Israelite religious beliefs.

As the dialogue continues between the serpent and the woman, the matter of man's divinity is presented by the serpent in verse 5 when the serpent says, "For God doth know that in the day ye eat thereof, then your eyes shall be opened, and ye shall be as gods, knowing good and evil." KJV. The

---

[25] Zondervan, *NIV Archaeological Study Bible: An Illustrated Walk-Through Biblical History and Culture*, not ed. (Grand Rapids: Zondervan, 2006),8.

word gods in this verse according to Strong's implies deity, divinity, and angels.[26] The irony of this portion of the story is that God had previously stated that man has been created in His Image. But what does it mean to be created in the image and likeness of God? According to Terry Mortenson, "The Image of God consists of the spiritual part of humankind that reflects the character of God."[27] In this, we recognize that man's spiritual being represents the part of his being that is as the Image of God and not his flesh because God does not possess a physical body. It is evident by the language of the serpent that it had knowledge of the nature of man. When we wish to express the image of God in Humanity, we should realize that we are discussing a matter that involves principle and idea, God is the root or principle of man's existence and man as the pure self of 1 John 3:3 is the idea of the being God "Imagined Man to Be".

It must be stated that there is substantial evidence biblically and extra biblically that modern man, nor those

---

[26]James Strong, *The New Strong's Exhaustive Concordance of the Bible: With Main Concordance, Appendix to the Main Concordance, Topical Index to the Bible, Dictionary of the Hebrew Bible, Dictionary of the Greek Testament* (Nashville, Tenn.: Thomas Nelson Inc, 1990),8.

[27] Dr Terry Mortenson, *Searching for Adam: Genesis and the Truth About Man's Origin*: Master Books, 2016),196.

before us really knows the substance nor precise make up of man. Paul writes in 1 Corinthians 12; "For now we see in a mirror, darkly; but then face to face: now I know in part; but then shall I know fully even as also I was fully known." ASV. But then shall I know fully even as also I was fully known is the point of focus for this writer's above statement that no one knows the substance of man. Paul is addressing the Corinthians, allowing the fact to be known that there exists a description of or knowledge of man's being that is fully known by God of which man will only come to perceive. That image and knowledge exists in the present but understanding of the manifestation according to Paul, does not.

The serpent seemed to have a greater understanding of the identity of man than even Paul. The serpent perceived that whatever the form of man at that time, man could become or transform. To gain a clearer understanding of this statement, consider the thoughts of other ancient cultures concerning the nature of man. The ancient Egyptians were a people highly concerned with their souls and the afterlife. They believed that there were three divisions of man which consisted of the ba, ka and akh. The ba originally described the power possessed by a god and permitted him to assume any form. Later, the ba came to represent a soul that animated the body of the dead man and enabled him to have life after death. Thus, making it necessary to preserve the body so that one will have a body after death. The Christian religion holds that the dead who goes to heaven will get a new body. Next is the ka which represents the vital force, a spiritual element present during life and after death. The final principle of the man was the akh, or the spiritual state achieved after death. Our point of reference to the statement of the serpent, "ye shall be as gods" however is the ba which was the power of the god to change its form. What we have seen is that the serpent was responsible in part for the fall of man in that it enticed the woman and she reasoned that she would gain wisdom from eating but by doing so, she disobeyed the command of God.

    Duane E. Smith in his article titled The Divining Snake: Reading Genesis 3 in the Context of Mesopotamian Ophiomancy goes so far as to state, that the serpent had secret powers of divination.[28] This student does not support the belief of Smith but feels that this helps the reader to understand more clearly, the beliefs concerning the nature of the serpent. Smith further states that he forms his conclusion based on Israel's knowledge of and pagan beliefs in divination

---

[28] Duane E. Smith, "The Divining Snake: Reading Genesis 3 in the Context of Mesopotamian Ophiomancy." The ATLAS collection, the American Theological Library Association. JBL 134. 1 (2015): 31-49 doi: http://dx.doi.org/10.15699/jbl.1341.2015.2757

as seen in the bible. Not only did the woman eat from the tree but she gave some of its fruit to the man and he also ate. It was not long after they consumed the fruit of the tree that they both recognized the results of disobedience. They realized that they were naked with a shameful nakedness, the kind of shame which led them to hide from God. Which is evidence of their spiritual decline and broken fellowship with God. We now come to the question presented by God to the man. God asked the man after the man had hidden himself, "Who told thee that thou wast naked?" This knowledge was the result of the new wisdom the man and woman now possessed. However, some do not perceive this wisdom as evil but contrast this wisdom with the wisdom of Solomon. "Finally, the connection between wisdom (specifically, kingly wisdom) and "knowing good and evil" is found in King Solomon's prayer in 1 Kgs 3:9. Give your servant therefore an understanding mind to govern your people, able to discern between good and evil."[29]

However, Genesis does not agree with this form of wisdom as being spiritual discernment but to the contrary, representing wickedness resulting in man's fall from fellowship with God. The fact that the man hid himself amongst the trees

---

[29] William N. Wilder, "The Royal Significance of the Tree of Wisdom in Genesis 3" The ATLAS collection, the American Theological Library Association. W7J68 (2006): 51-69

of the garden further highlights his spiritual and physical fall. By his association with inanimate trees rather than with God, Adam had become or taken on a different form just as the serpent stated. Now that Adam and Eve are no longer able to perceive of themselves as does God, it appears as if they have agreed through their acts of shame that they are worthy of punishment. Starting with the serpent in verse 14, God's judgement is pronounced. The woman used the word beguiled to describe what the serpent had done. Strong's uses delude as a synonym for beguile denoting that what the woman accused the serpent of was more than misleading her by means of casual conversation but that the serpent seduced her with an imposing belief. Not just a belief but a form of doctrinal or religious belief. As we examine further what God says to the serpent in verse 15, we notice the use of the words bruise thy head but when it comes to the enmity between the offspring of the woman and the serpent, the word it instead of the pronouns he or she is used in relation to the woman's seed. God says, "it shall bruise thy head, and thou shalt bruise his heel." Attention has shifted from the seed of the serpent to the serpent causing the bruising of the heel. This is here highlighted because the serpent is the head of the rebellion against God.

APPLICATION

It is the word of truth by which we overcome the world. Eve should have confronted the serpent with the truth of God's command. What the serpent did from the beginning was to cause the woman to doubt her identity. Once she began to doubt herself according to who God said she and Adam were, she gave the serpent the opportunity to make the tree the center of Attention. What we attend to with our minds, we give life. Life comes from Spirit and Adam has authority to give life to inanimate objects. The woman does not appear to have wanted to disobey God as much as she wanted to gain wisdom. The moral lesson however is that true wisdom comes from God only. One point of interest is that God never told them that they were naked, but the man told God that he was naked. This identifies the conscience of the man in the form of a type of conviction. God came back just as He had done in the past to fellowship with Adam as if nothing had changed as evidenced by God's question, "where are you?" and then, "who told you that you are naked?" Adam however was unable to perceive or understand with spiritual discernment because he had died. This type of death allowed Adam to continue to exist just as sinful man today continues to live a physical life. He is now alive to the world but dead in his knowledge of and relationship with God because his not God's imagination of himself fell. The physical form of man did not change but his Image was marred by "his own mind" and he became what he thought! We become what we think about!

Since the serpent was the reason for the downfall of the first man, then we are right to also blame everyone else except ourselves for our failures. Not the lack of planning, and as Napoleon Hill puts so succinctly, not the lack of "self-control", will and power, power being: Organized Knowledge expressed through Intelligent Efforts, not the man's own will but a "Serpent", a creature, a creeping crawling thing over which Adam had authority. Yes, maybe Adam was right, it was a "Serpent"; the deceived, the marred, soulless image of man, (soulless because God is not his creator) crawling on his belly eating dust when he should be ruling dust, get it "Ruling Dust". Man, created from dust should first be ruler of himself; shaper of the dust, forming and shaping what he believes into reality, tangible matter, as it exists in his mind. ("The Potter" of his own wheel) This should be familiar:

"If anyone does not know how to manage his own household, how will he take care of God's church?" 1Timothy 3.

Everything in a man's house should only reside within because the ruler of the house says so. This Garden experience and the fall of man clearly expresses a state of man's psyche and identifies vividly the constant struggle within himself to understand himself! The reality in which we now live is the entire garden scene expressed in a seemingly new and different time but is only revealing an epoch or state in which man must pass in the evolution of his revealed identity. Paul explains the evolution by stating "I die daily." The woman and the man were cast out of the garden: "Each individual human being possess forces, within himself that are hard to harmonize, even when he is placed in the environment most favorable" Napoleon Hill. If he is not a harmonized being, he will be "cast out".

How can the two, Adam and Eve walk together unless they agree? And who are the two except that they become one mind and be known by what they Create as God is known only by His Creation. When the house is destroyed by a fire, the two must stand out in the cold. When the house is divided against itself, the house is ablaze. What then is this chapter about? Cognitive Dissonance: Does Man possess the Nature of God or Serpent? I was taken from Pure God, but a man told me that I am full of hell, and I have been manifesting what I believe ever since I heard a Serpent speak…

ADAM Man Convoluted but GOD

Man Does Not Have To Go To Heaven…

"The Lord God said, "Since man has become like one of Us, knowing good and evil, he must not reach out, take from the tree of life, eat, and live forever" … HCSB

And Jehovah God saith, "Lo, the **man was as one of Us,** *as to the knowledge of good and evil; and now, lest he send forth his hand, and have taken also of the tree of life, and eaten, and lived to the age"* … YLT

Man created in the Image of God, created with the faculties to know just as God knows, possessing the ability to change his identity but lacking the gift of eternal life. To understand this convoluted man, he must be dissected, he must be given multiple identities according to his "separate and divided Nature". To understand this religious man, Adam must be made to believe that what he eats relegates his nature, he must believe that eternal life comes from what he eats and what he does can affect who he was from the beginning. If we are concerned with the end of man, we should be more concerned with his beginning. Great minds have contemplated Who is

Man, and what is his substance? I would like to consider a point of entry into the conversation by defining terms associated with theories of Man's origin. Before I introduce terms, I will attempt to preface my thought with a verse from the book of Revelation: **"Let the filthy go on being made filthy; and let the holy go on being made holy."** 22:11 As I begin to revolutionize this scripture into the evolution of man, I am aware of the resistance which may come as a result of my use of the words "being made". Someone will say this interpretation takes the scripture out of context; his use of it is semantically incorrect... I could pause here for a moment and exchange wits, but I rather continue to write and let the meaning unroll and develop as you continue to read. Since this chapter concerns living in Heaven or dying to get there, two types of thought by default are introduced: The Evolutionist and Fundamentalist.

"It was known then, for example, that the atmosphere of the earth, with its plentiful supply of oxygen, was not present in the early years of our solar system, and that it developed only because unicellular organisms in the primeval sea had discovered how to use photosynthesis to feed themselves, thus producing a surplus of oxygen that, over the course of a billion years or so, created an atmosphere in which multicellular life – plants, animals, and others could begin to inhabit the land masses that had previously been barren rocks." *Religion in Human Evolution, pg. xi.* The early years of the Solar System in Bellah's book references a period before the earth could sustain Man; only a one celled organism from the Primeval Sea could live and this ability afforded by the Photosynthesis or Power of the Sun to have life and thus Give Life to the organism! In the beginning, God said… At a set time God said, Life can begin… Who created the Atmosphere for these multicellular organisms? Whom do we believe creates the Atmosphere for this complex evolving Life? Who causes his Life to become complex? The Power of the Word! Indeed, it is the Power of the Word that makes him! The first word in understanding Man is Revolution: *the action by a <u>celestial body</u> of going round in an orbit or <u>elliptical course</u>… Also, from revolvere '***roll back***'.* Stay with me, I am getting ready to pick up the pace!

God said to the man and woman, **Replenish** the Earth. The second word is Evolution: **unrolling**, *from the verb evolvere Early senses related to movement, first recorded in describing a 'wheeling' maneuver in the <u>realignment of troops or ships</u>.* Man is evolving on an elliptical course: deliberate obscurity. Since the desire is to live in Heaven after death, we must find out where he existed before Life.

God blessed them and said "Be fruitful" I have given you every Seed-Bearing Plant on the surface of the entire earth and every tree whose fruit contains this Seed of Life. The first command and lesson given to man was the **Fecundity** of the Seed. But this command given to man concerning fruitfulness according to Christian theology could not have the contemporary meaning for seed today, for the seed we know today must first die (so says the Dead Man) so that it may produce life. Foolish one! What you sow does not come to life unless it dies. This was seed from a different fruit, for death is the result of sin and man had not yet sinned therefore fruit did not die but was Life for man. Does the seed have to die to produce life or is the fruit the result of a seed transformed? But in a world where death was unknown, why then the need for seed producing fruit trees? What we call death is also the transformation into the highest form of life; So also, He has granted to the Son to have life in Himself, therefore, the Father is in the Son. Did not these fruit trees have sustaining life in them? God gave the Man every green plant, every plant that was able to transform within itself the energy of the Sun. Eating from this tree would also cause the Son in Man to live. So, man does not have to die to live, he only must eat that which has life.

So far, we have been concerned with what the man ate to cause him to die but what would have become of the man if he would not have eaten any food at all, would life remain in him for death was not yet known? Man, then must eat or he will die and since he has eaten the food of man, he is afraid to be Immortal. The story has been interpreted by a mortal man who's life is death. Let Adam eat food for his body, for the Spiritual Man does not come from dirt and that which he was in the beginning, he will always be… God, neither made nor unmade except that he has been made filthy in his own mind. So therefore, let the filthy go on being made filthy and let the holy go on being made holy. Each man has the right to see in himself what he wills. What he sees, will be made outside of himself. If he has seen a mansion, he will build a mansion, he will become that which He Believes He is Filthy, let him become what he wills.

The process of rebirth begins with the question; What beginning? And contemplating this reasoning, the idea of "Heaven and Hell" is promulgated by the builders of man. To entertain the idea of heaven and hell, the concept of duality must be considered and accepted. Eating from that one fruit tree caused the man to consume more than what he could swallow, and his children's teeth are set on edge from its bitterness. Is man a complete/congruent being or is he dual? By duality, I speak in terms of religious thought: "the old me and the new me", the 1st Adam and the 2nd Adam according to Paul. If we were to be led on a journey, we would gain an idea of the terrain, mode of travel, and destination of our travels by carefully paying attention to the requirements of the packing list. To understand one's present condition, he must unpack the concepts upon which are built his beliefs become words become actions become the total sum of the man. From the religious belief, God accepts the new me and opposes the old me, therefore the old me is not from God and must die and a new me must be born, comes a hell for the old man and a heaven for the new. In psychology, a concept is defined as the building blocks of thought. But just because a person holds a thought in his mind does not indicate that he has used the thinking process to analyze the building blocks of the thought. Conclusions and concepts are similar in that both involve a process of reasoning and that both are relative and may not be formed or substantiated by truth but instead may be affected by superstitious belief, ignorance, and fear.

It is not until the Wine runs out that the source of intoxication is understood. Wine is the simplest form of leavened natural sugar in grapes. To get wine, a process of fermentation must take place, before fermentation, the seed, the soil, and the climate must be considered if quality wine is desired. However, the wine is but a byproduct of a process, a principle. The altered molecules of the grapes produce an intoxicating substance and when ingested, alter the thoughts which in turn alters the behavior of the consumer. When the wine is gone, the man returns to his senses, he is free from the effects of the intoxicant. The host who serves the wine uses psychological manipulation when he serves the better wine at first then replacing it with the inferior after the intoxicating principle has caused a reaction within the man. It is no longer the man who is consciously acting but the principle in him forcing him to react. What he drinks is not the whole fruit, but fruit altered by the mind of the alchemist. The wine is the agent, the man is the subject, and the purpose of the Gardener is to identify the man, the fruit of the field. He is fermented, his desire has identified his nature, he is therefore reduced to his most basic and natural state, his Nature has been identified. The grapes neither the wine was the subject but the servants themselves have been identified. In simple terms, Adam's wife; his Nature was beguiled because they were twain... Wrong concepts causes the man to live a life divided, separated from his true self; old skins reject "New Wine". It was the servants for whom the wine was prepared. In the old man's thinking, he must die, the new man has only a renewing of his mind and says, "Let the dead bury their own." Those intoxicated beings of man!

Now that you fully understand and can properly rearrange molecules so that what you ingest will be wholesome food, for you now understand that it is not what goes into a man but what comes out of him and what comes forth from him is the Agent who speaks of the fermented fruit, his "Nature" is that of the serpent who beguiles.

Concerning the promulgation of heaven and hell What part since he is divided does the beginning apply? God who has neither beginning nor end brought forth Adam from within Himself, (Christ the "begotten") which part of God has a beginning? None, "In the Beginning" simply implies God as the Principle of all that Is, came from Him, He is the "Principle of Life"...To begin to understand this convoluted man, we must contemplate a God who is also divided, a god who creates from different hemispheres of his human brain,[30] some for noble purposes and some for base. The Man who became as the result of a first thought, has arrived and his mind is his vehicle... The **mind** seated in the innermost brain, the priest of the soul who rules the body, the boney protective structure, the ark of the covenant... The Mind is the set of cognitive faculties, the Man is a thinking being. Man is a thinking being are not just idle words put together as rhetoric, "Man is a being of thought". He came from an eternal thought. His entire being, who he is and will become are based solely on principle

---

[30] Anthropomorphism

and what he contemplates. Let me explain, when a man is given a book, the book causes him to consider intensely, not just passive consideration of its pages but to become consumed by the power of spirit in the words.

The purpose of the introduction is to engage the mind and appeal to a particular congregation, a specific audience possessing a like mind with that of the author. Once stimulated and engaged, the setting is introduced and this is where the reader leaves the confines of physical space and time and travels by means of mental levitation, elevated by the power of imagination to a different place and time, he is placed in the magical garden of thought. Not only is he introduced to characters in the setting, but he also relates to and becomes a part of the setting, he is one of its subjects, he becomes one with the creator. The plot causes him to take thought of his own life's experiences, he is fully engaged, flesh and spirit, a living soul; one in thought. Then comes moments of confusion where reality and the imaginary, literal and allegory coexist introducing conflict, Day and Night, Darkness and Light and masters of two creations which brings us to death and dying. Products, subjects and children of conflict and irrational thinking, unable to distinguish Life from death or in other words, "I came that you might have life" but I cannot and will not have a good life until I die. How do we get death from the concept of life? What is the sum of 1 + 0? 1 + 0 is the sum of the Lie of Good and Evil. There is Only God...

This divided man who believes that he must die so that he can live in heaven; let him first understand the Man who lives: John 3:12-13 If I have told you about things that happen on earth and you do not believe, how will you believe if I tell you about things of heaven? **No one has ascended into heaven except the One who descended from heaven the Son of Man.** *All Life comes from Heaven, the Higher Ether; Breath of God...*

It is not in heaven so that you have to ask, 'Who will go up to heaven, get it for us...

Then again in Isaiah 51:16 God says, "And I have put my words in thy mouth, and **I have covered thee in the shadow of mine hand, that I may plant the heavens**, and lay the foundations of the earth, and say unto Zion, Thou art my people." May you accept here what you can believe and live by. Remember, not all of us benefit from the same diet. Some men are vegan, some vegetarian and some meat eaters, may you not be judged by man for what you live on. Let your diet consist of those things which benefit and not destroy. Listen carefully, I have covered thee in the shadow of my hand, **that I may plant the heavens.** Where were you when God planted the heavens?

This quote comes word for word from the book Basic

Theology by Charles Ryrie, *"Eternality means not only that Christ existed before His birth or even before Creation but that He existed always, eternally."*

  God does not have hands like man, when God plants, He speaks, when He spoke, man was hidden in the shadow-unseen Power of the Word of God; Man was with God in the beginning when the Word was made known from Heaven. Heaven is planted in the Man for that man alone knows where is heaven from which He came. Let the dead bury the dead for the man who lives cannot die for Christ is his eternal Principle. So, let the filthy go on being made filthy, and the holy go on being made holy as he is what he thinks he is, he can know no other reality! Son of Man, the life you live, you spoke into existence since you were with God in the beginning. The foundations were laid for you, that which you have on earth, you knew in heaven, if it were not so for you in heaven, it is impossible for you on earth. Hidden in the shadow of the hand of God earth was created for your life which was hidden in heaven to be revealed in the life you Now Live! The earth is waiting in eager expectation for the Sons of God to be revealed, for the earth is Mine and I will reap its Harvest! Man does not have to die to go… He can be if he so desires. Adam you were with God, He said you were in the beginning… But, since you have been told about the end, let us define

Eschatology: this part of theology concerned with death.

When the Sun rises in the morning, a new day has dawned, darkness has passed, and the fear of the unseen does not terrify the uncivilized man for old things are gone and he can see himself clearly. He can only see according to his Sun that rises on the Horizon... Does the man who is dead know that death exists? No because he believes that death is life... Listen, Solomon said, "The dead know Nothing." Now listen to the mystical words of Christ, "For when they rise from the dead, they neither marry nor are given in marriage but are like angels in heaven."

Now concerning the dead being raised, haven't you read in the book of Moses, in the passage about the burning bush, how God spoke to him: I am the God of Abraham and the God of Isaac and the God of Jacob? He is not God of the dead but of the living. You are badly deceived." Christ, if I may explain to the people for you have given me eyes to see and ears to hear and I AM ALIVE, for God knows who I AM. Those who rose were not dead but those who were concerned with death were already dead, you will see this if you listen to their conversations. God is not God of the dead but of the living, the man who comes from God is Life, how can he be dead if he rises? When you talk to the Man of Life, He is likened unto Elohim for He is risen above the dead and they know not! Those who are alive know nothing, but Life and God is in Him. Those who must die to go to heaven are already dead, Heaven seems far from them. They talk about those who are there but are badly deceived... Who they are cannot be understood for they speak of them (the heavenly beings) from an earthly perspective.

The Abstract Phenomenon of Death is only relative to the living. Attempting to understand death and the possibility of life after death, one must start with what is being considered. If death is to be considered, it is only done so by the living. A newlywed virgin does not grieve for her unconceived, unknown child. The dead do not mourn but the living who has known life. Those who grieve, do not grieve for gain...
(Heaven) but for loss. Who can say that he really knows love if his wish is to withhold the righteousness of completion from the one, he loves? The meaning of death as expressed by the living is an emotional response to perceived loss; Is the unconceived child dead or not yet made alive? Do those made alive, die into a different existence than those who never existed but are dead to the living? Death has meaning for the living for the dead know nothing unless he was first known. Life then gives meaning to death, and if this is true, that which is unknown is eternal and that which has been made known is temporary. The perceived loss is the lack of understanding and

that which was to be gained by the living has been misunderstood.

Life misunderstood is The Abstract Phenomenon of Life perceived by the dead. The expressions life and death are axioms used to conceptualize infinite Man. Infinite because he was not dead in the beginning. If he was not dead in the beginning, he shall not be dead in the end for neither exist. Hell has been created for the man who was brought forth from the bliss of death for life was unknown to him. His life was in God, he was not self for only God knew Him, for since God alone knew Him, was God's thoughts of Him considered evil? Is the Self evil, is He continually becoming and after evolving what does He manifest, Good or Evil, where is His home, Heaven or Hell?

When the farmer beheld the seed in his hand, did he perceive the Harvest? Did he gain his sustenance from the seed, or did he create conditions favorable for the seed to become? He must first know the seed… The Farmer not the tree is made known by the fruit of the field, the tree is made of wood, life is in the fruit; God was once in an Ark made of wood; Convoluted Man, that Arcane place of God has evolved… The seed could not become that which he never was, for Life has always been in Him. Since life has always been, how does he also know death for although He was not known, He was Also alive but in a shell! He becomes that which he Wills, and he will have an abundance in Heaven or in Hell exists in Him, He makes it known; but from him who has not, even what he has will be taken away for it never existed, his works were not known in Heaven; the organism creates the conditions for His evolution, He has been given the Earth, and on this earth, we "raise up" children in the way they should go.

Learning starts at an incredibly young age, possibly before birth which causes loving parents to pay special attention to the child's atmosphere and environment, especially what the child eats, knowing that a growing person needs a balanced diet to perpetuate good health. In fact, for those mothers who are very conscious of the importance of balanced nutrition, they breast feed their infants with the same milk and life force from within their own bodies and would not dare to think about going to the nearest market traveling down a long isle of synthetic milks modified in a laboratory then bringing these substitutes home to feed her innocent baby. No, the mother who is conscious and has planned birth by participating in child development courses knows that there is nothing that man may invent that can take the place of (first milk), the first form of milk produced by the mammary glands of mammals (including many humans) immediately following delivery of the newborn. ... **Colostrum** contains antibodies to protect the newborn against disease. The most significant fact of colostrum which relates to this chapter of the book is that when ingested, it strengthens the child's "immune system": **the body's defense system against harmful bacteria.** It has been said that nothing can come between a mother's love for her child and that the woman of the smallest stature gets the strength of a bull when her child is in danger! Transitioning into the subject of dying to live in heaven, why does this strong mother get weak when it comes to religious doctrines formed as the foundation of her child's eternal destiny.

In religious institutions and loving homes, it is mandated that responsible parents should involve their young children in some form of "Sunday School" class either in the home or at the family's church. One side note, more and more religious leaders are getting away from using the phrase Sunday School but have coined the phrase "Church School" or "The Lord's Day School". What has brought about this change of thought? Back to the subject as you ponder the reasoning behind that question.

John Dewey in his book, "The Child and The Curriculum" writes, *"Profound differences in theory are never gratuitous or invented. They grow out of conflicting elements in a genuine problem, a problem which is genuine just because the elements, taken as they stand, are conflicting. Any significant problem involves conditions that for the moment contradict each other. Solution comes only by getting away from the meaning of terms that is already fixed upon and coming to see the conditions from another point of view, and hence in a fresh light. But this reconstruction means travail of thought. Easier than thinking with surrender of already formed ideas and detachment from facts already learned, is just to stick by what is already said, looking about for something with which to buttress it against attack. Thus, sects arise, schools of Opinion. Each selecting the set of conditions that appeal to it; and then solidifying their opinions into a complete and independent truth, instead of treating them as a factor in a problem, needing adjustment."*

The original Sin doctrine teaches that man born of woman is a sinner from birth and is therefore dead and will continue dying an eternal death until he is born again. Not only that, but everything he does as a sinner, is as works of the wicked, worthy of the fire, for there is no good in him, no matter what good works of charity he participates in. This the good spiritual colostrum and foundation on which our children are cultured, believing that they are children of the devil, their mothers and fathers evidently are the devil since they give birth to devils. No one asks the question; well since the mother and father are born again, receiving the DNA of Christ having the same Spirit and Life of Christ through rebirth, how can the child reach back to a different DNA?

May they all be one, as You, Father, are in Me and I am in

You. May they also be one in Us, so the world may believe You sent Me. ***I have given them the glory You have given Me.*** *May they be one as We are one. I am in them, and You are in Me. May they be made completely one...* John 17:21-23.

If a "Man Is As He Thinketh", there is no wonder that the Earth, not somewhere beneath the Earth's crust but the World that man's ideas have created is the Hell that Christ went down to wrestle the keys of bondage away from Satan in the presence of a multitude of witnesses. The witnesses are those whose minds are transformed by the truth of the real message of Christ and this Earth is the stage set by the thoughts of Man. By the way, God gave man the keys in the beginning.

"Therefore, it logically follows that this system of treatment is for the purpose of uncovering and neutralizing the wrong states of thought... of building in mind a concept of our spiritual birthright. Thought which is built upon a realization of the Divine Presence has the power to neutralize negative thought, to erase it, just as light has the power to overcome darkness; not by combating darkness, but by being exactly what it is: LIGHT. **"And the light shineth in the darkness; and the darkness comprehended it not."** *The Science of Mind pg. 183*

Do not let the Concept of Death intrigue you! Whatever the concept is... if it does not relate to your Spiritual Birthright, it is against your purpose, an obstacle placed by carnal thinking. **The Minister**

A great mind once said, "The problem with men is that they don't think."

The problem with men is that they think in a controlled environment. In fact, men in a controlled environment will continue to cause the environment to stay the same. Since the environment is the same, what is seen is the same, what is thought is the same, what is spoken of is the same, and because of what is spoken, their actions are the same although the men change and begin to see things differently, still, the environment does not change! When the conversation changes, someone from the grave says, "Dream On!"

If I Have Not Life!...

With whom then am I speaking if I have not life? Where am I? I am thinking, but what is thought? Who said that!? Someone is speaking to me ... Who am I and where did I come from? I have a body but what is a body? I see things moving what are these? Who put me here? Get back animal are you here to devour me? I spoke to that lion, and he moved away, I was hungry and picked a round thing from the great big green and brown thing and I am not hungry anymore. I AM! But I cannot be for I have not eaten from that tree with the dazzling lights, the brightest tree of the field. I keep hearing a Voice, there is someone else here, someone I cannot see, He is inside of me; and He Is Heaven... But my mind is In Hell...

The Detriment of Religious Dogma and Promulgation of Fear...

So that the stage may be set, before you begin this chapter, I will present a statement in the form of a question for the reader to contemplate, a thesis statement, a statement of engagement to entice your interest in case the title does not. It is a simple question, one in which not many people consider although it is in the first three chapters of the Bible. 1ˢᵗ God never introduced the serpent by name to the man and woman. 2ⁿᵈ The Bible never states that the man ever saw the serpent, or the "Forbidden Tree" and 3ʳᵈ How did the man know that the fruit being an "apple" according to popular but outdated thought, was from the forbidden tree and not an "apple" from the "Tree of Life"? Since the man and all his generations after him were affected by what he himself did not see, hear, talk to, etc.… was only made known to him by his "wife" or (subconscious mind). God is "One" Spirit, from whom only righteousness comes…There are diseases, deformities, sicknesses, and mental illness affecting the lives of many in our present world today. This author had an uncle who once had an extremely high temperature and started to hallucinate. Believing that there were large animals in the room, he started to exclaim, "Get back! Do you see that over there, Get back!" As he was yelling, in a state of panic and fear, sweating and confused, everyone else in the room was unaffected except for experiencing the drama played out by a "sick man". The reality of a feverish, delusional mind! Ask yourself, "Am I living in the drama of a sick man"? Every tree that the Lord God planted in the garden was good for food... Genesis 2:9. No animal named by the man in the garden was his compliment, so God caused the man to fall into a deep sleep; meditation... To awaken his subconscious mind so that he could imagine, "Make Believe". To see what God already knew...

Some readers may not follow this idea of "Awakening the subconsciousness of man" you may even feel that the thought is unscriptural. Before moving forward, consider this scene from the Bible: Mark 4:38-40 paying attention to the part of the ship where Jesus slept, then verse 40, Jesus asked them why the lack of faith. Not faith in him as some may suggest. He was addressing their lack of faith in the power of the Word he had been teaching them. They themselves were asleep or as Paul states: "Fan into flame the Gift of God within you". Christ was fanning into flame the part of them that slept, the

ADAM Man Convoluted but GOD

"Subconscious, Spiritual Man", the 2nd Adam with his wife to whom he is joined, he could **imagine:** make manifest from a mental image/an idea/a seed, into a world of his own! He no longer had to live in God's world, he could experience a world relative to his own belief produced from experience. He was free-at Liberty to "Make Believe" out of God's Word what he could perceive as reality for himself, and it would be so. A world of experience, just as the woman's experience was suggested to the man, he took and ate, and her world became his. His world did not change because of what he gained from participatory experience but was the result of what was given to him to consume. It was the passion and spirit gained from the fruit that changed the man's reality. It was what he thought/imagined about the fruit offered, it was his perception that changed his reality. The woman gave him an idea forged by her mind, he made the fruit of the tree food, and his life was changed by a serpent who was a lie in God's world!

    The question we are left to consider is this; Where did the man get the capacity to imagine anything other than righteousness? In other words, before the woman gave the man the food, he could choose, there was a suggestion of the idea or possibility of dual spirits: Good and Evil, Death and Life before he ate. The astute student of scripture would exclaim at the last statement, "God did not announce Good and Evil only Life and Death!" Where did the man get the idea that life was anything except the righteousness of Life and Death? Both Trees the Lord God Planted were Good for Food: for the Spiritual man and earthly man, one body. To examine the Hebrew word for food would add clarity to the above Genesis scripture. "He humbled you by letting you go hungry; then He gave you **manna** to eat, which you and your fathers had **not** known, so that you might learn that **man does not live** on bread alone but on every word that comes from the mouth of the Lord. This man described here in Deuteronomy is not two but one, although he does eat manna and bread… Not only does this man eat, but he also has the authority to turn that which is not Food into Bread? The same tempter/idea from the garden confronted Christ suggesting that Man has the authority to satisfy his hunger with the Lie… To examine the Hebrew word for food would add clarity to the sentences above. Once examined, think deeper, and consider what portion is beneficial for the priest to eat… To burn up… While reading the Book of Genesis, Moses is ministering to the earthly man as well as the Spiritual man, the Sheep eats as well as the Goat, and they both receive their fill for their journey, for their destiny… Now that the Stage is set, let us break bread together and have our fill.

After the exile, many Jews continued to miss the

fullness of God's Word, specifically the Lord's grace. Since even many of the Jews in Babylon before the restoration thought that their expulsion from Canaan meant that our Creator takes pleasure in sinners' deaths (Ezek. 18:23), it was hard for the post-exilic community to believe the Lord had not utterly abandoned them, especially since the glorious post-exilic restoration did not immediately occur. Joshua the High Priest spoken of in Zechariah's vision in chapter 3, has been identified by some as a fore shadowing of Christ. The question is, however, what in this scripture is representative of the coming Christ? For the Bible says, "So the Angel of the Lord spoke to those standing before Him, "Take off his filthy clothes!" Then He said to him, "See, I have removed your guilt from you, and I will clothe you with splendid robes." It does not say see, I have removed the guilt of the world, those sinners you died for from you but says explicitly; "See, I have removed your guilt from you." Filthy clothes literally mean soiled as if by human excrement. Well, cleaning the outside of a cup is to whitewash the contents within and furthermore, man is not defiled by what goes into him but by what proceeds from him, his excrement. Not urine or feces but what he takes into him, his beliefs revealed by word revealed by actions; what he does on earth, the life he lives causes defilement exposing his belief system.

ADAM Man Convoluted but GOD

Too often we are so anxious to see Jesus in scripture that the message for man is lost. Joshua represents those coming out of the Babylonian captivity as he was one of the first. The superstitious Israelites ruled by "inverted faith", otherwise known as fear, believed that God takes pleasure in destroying sinners. However, this scripture gives multiple examples of grace towards man and illustrates the image of God in man, namely: Spirit/Priest in the order of Melchizedek, the incorruptible seed: Christ who could never sin, for sin is a lie formed in the mind of man rooted in his fear of being like God. Satan standing there was also from Joshua's belief system. (Satan comes with the man as his own consciousness.) God does not accuse the man, the man takes his fearful belief system and religion into God's presence, as did Adam when he hid himself. Let us consider God being moved by a spirit outside Himself? How could God recognize evil as anything except a lie?

In other words, evil is not a problem to God, the problem of evil comes in man as a petrified *(within his own mind)* concept. It is not a matter of how God responds to the individual but how the individual responds in contemplation of his concept of himself. Man is fearful of his own righteousness and is unable to rationalize his own perfection. There are only two types of people on this earth; those who are good and those who do not recognize that they are good. Every animal created has the ability and does function within the "Right Concept" of itself. Every animal is perfect according to the perfect idea from which it was created. Man is also perfect, for he is the perfect idea of God and could be nothing less than that idea. However, man is at liberty with a free will to live a life of less than, a life of misery and poverty. Not only is this a fact but is promulgated by his spiritual belief system. Just as God in the mind of the lesser man lives outside of himself, so does the savior live outside of the lesser man. For the Divine Spirit to reside in a man-made box is perfectly acceptable, the same in man is beyond contemplation. The box made by the hands of man is holy, the heart fashioned by God un-holy…

This man clothed in garments weaved by inferior fabric wears a robe that is stained by human excrement: (etymology) to sift out; to sieve, to distinguish. The result of reduction or deduction: man's reasoning as he handled the pure truth; sifted through the theology of man; the crumbs under the table fit for a dog has become his portion. Joshua, a man! Not Jesus of Nazareth but a man who walked the earth long before the remarkable incarnation should cause the realization of the spiritual message to all men. God told Zechariah, also a man who we call a "prophet" as to distinguish his substance from our substance, the one substance. In the lesser man's eye Zechariah was a prophet and prophets only can hear from God? (Identification and conversation by the lesser man) Joshua the High Priest was likewise not a man but a foreshadowing of Christ. (Man does not and cannot perceive within himself perfection)

This chapter is titled, the detriment of religious dogma and promulgation of fear. Before we continue, the terms detriment and religious dogma must be understood. Religious dogma alone is not the detriment of man, but the promulgation of fear is. It is the opinion of this author that if a man's belief system does not set him free, elevating his consciousness, he cannot know God. For the quest of theology is that man should come into the knowledge of God. The knowledge of God made known to the world is the Image of Himself in man! "Know Thyself" and rejoice in the Lord. If this knowledge produces fear, detriment is revealed for man has received the "Mark of the Beast". Adam displayed this mark of fear when he contemplated God in the garden. Someone may say while reading this book, "This is the wrong understanding of the context of the Fear of God, or the fear which emanates from God. The author is aware of the Hebrew description of fear, the fear that comes from the bowels of God. Let me explain: Fear is the interpretation and the reality of a personal mind set affected by one's own irrational thought, as was that of those terrified by the Babylonian exile. The exile was not eternal punishment but a process of identification. Not realizing that it was fear exchanged for the knowledge of the Gift. The God they knew in the box was transformed into the God who lives in the Heart... They feared Growth...

Acquiescence of the Mind...

With reluctant acceptance, intelligent men and women have accepted error as wisdom and tradition as substitute for knowledge of themselves and understanding what "to be alive" really means. Accepting these traditions, our children have suffered the greatest harm, they have accepted superstitious fear as the Word of God. What then is the meaning of Acquiesce? And how can the infant protest? A question is only valid if it relates to the nature of the conversation. If the listener does not have knowledge of the subject of the conversation, his question will reveal his ignorance and he will cease to ask questions, thus accepting what he does not understand. Protest comes when one is confronted with conflicting information, when his reality is threatened, his innate instinct of self-preservation causes him to challenge the threat. If there is no sense of threat, there is no need to challenge, and if I believe that I fully understand, I refuse to appear as a child. Not only will the intelligent refuse to eat with the foolish, but I will also only accept those who live in my World of Understanding. Living in this world, I do what I do not understand, but surely, I understand because what I have learned to do, keeps me alive in this world! So therefore, I keep on doing what keeps me alive and the world will never change...

Those things which I do not know, I do, and if you are my child, you do what I tell you to do for what I tell you to do, I cannot understand. Do it anyway, for you are my child... Acquiescence of the Mind introduces us to a practice or ritual practiced a long time ago. Yes, practiced and now perfected! What was once called sacrifice of the innocent has now become the Silence of the Lambs... Acquiescence of the Mind. If you are familiar with the Bible at all, you may have read or at least heard in church talk about causing children to pass through the fire. If you have heard of this practice, then you have probably thought about this practice as literally burning children as religious dedication to God. Maybe not burning as an offering to the True God but practiced in recognition of a god in the name of God for they believed that God required this. So therefore, if I do what I believe god wants then I am serving the True God... Acquiescence of the Mind... The God I serve is known by what I do when I serve him... If I cause my children to do what I do not understand, I yet practice the ritual of causing my children to pass through the Fire.

Sacrifice in this case does not infer literal sacrifice but rather, the building of a foundation from which, the end has already been predicted. We know the end because the life you now live is not your own if you believe what they believe and do what they do, they have already predicted you because you were caused to pass through their Fire. The fire is the Light… and the light is the revelation! Accepting another man's limitations as the revelation, limits you! You will only accomplish what he has, and he knows your destiny, for He alone has formed You…

(Mindfulness)

"The observer paints the picture!" He does not hear wisdom because he is distracted. He is distracted by what has been made obvious by the nature of the environment. What is made obvious is the idea which has become prevalent within a group of people who have agreed to unite. It is not until one is able to think about what and why he is thinking about what he is thinking that change can occur. To agree does not suggest careful forethought but I agree because it fits the mold, it supports the paradigm of the moment where I AM present. And where I am now, others are there agreeing with me. Adam hid amongst the trees because they looked like him. These people are there in body, but the mind is not present, Adam is caught in the atmosphere, he has lost his sense of time, he is one with his feelings of the atmosphere, his senses are ruling his mind.

Energy is infinite potential directed towards the accomplishment of a desired goal. The Concept of Adam has been distorted. Righteous Adam represented infinite potential. The observer gave to Adam his identity, while interpreting the story, the interpreter saw himself as a sinner, therefore Adam was not the Only Begotten Son. Was the man formed or was he made? Let Us Make Man into our image…

Let Us Make Man into our own likeness. Let Us take infinite potential and create by the power of our own thoughts. Thought is the force by which matter is changed, Let us use the power of thought and make mankind clones of Adam, he was a sinner, and the rest are like him. Atom is empty, thought fills him, and thought gives him life. God made potential appear, man named him Adam. The Great Spirit brought to the man all the animals that he should name them… What means God made potential appear? He gave him life, he became aware, his eyes were opened, and he could see himself. The greatest and most powerful name above all names is that name to which the man answers. When he answers to that name, his world is created and everything that is created answers to him. All he believes, he creates. Nothing has been created by him unless he first believes in his name. He is not identified by the creation, the creation is identified by him, without him, his creation does not exist.

If your parents would not have told you that your name was Adam, would you have sinned? *(Have you been sacrificed to the fire?)* Would you be a victim of circumstance, controlled by the Genesis passed own to you? Sorry, that was a mistake on my part, I misspelled Genes, and I keep confusing Adam with Atom. Maybe, just maybe the two are related, intentionally or unintentionally, both are involved in the origin of things. Nothing that has been made was made without either. Gene - a unit of heredity which is transferred from a parent to offspring and is held to determine some characteristic of the offspring. Etymology of Gene - a supposed ultimate unit of heredity (from Greek *pan-* 'all' + *genos* 'race, kind, offspring'). The Book of Genesis – Race: *Mankind*; Then God said, "Let the earth produce living creatures according to their *kinds*: Livestock, creatures that crawl, and the wildlife of the earth according to their *kinds*." And it was so. Thus, the profound statement of Jesus, *"You are deceived, because you don't know the Scriptures or the power of God. For in the resurrection, they neither marry nor are given in marriage but are like angels in heaven."* Since they will not marry, will they also cease having offspring?

Two corrupt cells can create a world of corruption, but healthy and pure cells are not only sterile as in microbiology but are impotent as in Void of Life, for the Gene can no longer produce when it dies. So, here in lies the purpose of mentioning the death of the Gene: Life has been given to the Man to Live on Earth:

Now concerning the resurrection of the dead, haven't you read what was spoken to you by God: I am the God of Abraham and the God of Isaac and the God of Jacob? He is not the God of the dead, but of the living."

They have put them to sleep, those who live in the city streets, the commotion is their way of life and they have become masters of disturbance. The self that they know is not the self they observed with their own Mind. For the commotion in the streets has distracted them from the Awareness of his potential; the emptiness of the Atom *(You will find rest for yourselves. For My yoke is easy and My burden is light)* ... The Fire is the Light

    My Father would always tell me to "be Mindful Son!" of what I do Today and Today, 40 years later, I could finally hear wisdom calling out in those city streets he was warning me about... Have you really used your Mind to consider what my Burden is Light truly means? The only burden of man is to light up his space. He carries on him all the days of his life, the burden of light within himself. If wisdom cries out above the noise of commotion, why doesn't he hear? He has not heard, not because he cannot. Women yell as loud as they can in the direction of a man who appears as if his eyes are wide open, surely, he has heard her plea! Why then is he unmoved into action? She is yelling not because he did not hear, she is yelling because there is a disconnect… His presence, his state is governed by his mind. She calls him ignorant, how long foolish ones, will you love ignorance? Why ignorance? Isn't ignorance relative to one's awareness? He has been made ignorant by what he has loved, he has emptied himself of the truth to make room for the created woman, the wisdom of the world, the woman he saw on the corner, the corner of those city streets. And yet, the Government is on his shoulders, his mind governs the World… He is burdened when he refuses to Govern according to the light within him. (Remember now that good citizens must respond to the light, their parents have caused them to pass through the Fire!)

    Be Mindful of why you do what you do. What you do does not define who you are, what you do only identifies what you have been listening to in those city streets… Be Mindful, or your emptiness will be filled up… Be Mindful and the commotion will not penetrate you. I can now hear the words of my Father ever so clearly… The Government is My Own

Mind. The burden is not his to "live for me", but the burden is mine to illuminate those City streets. Regardless of who he believes himself to be, the center of his being will always be Him and he is expected to fulfill His potential. Everything exposed by the light is made clear, for what makes everything clear is light.

Therefore, it is said: Get up, sleeper, and "rise up" from the dead and the Messiah will shine on you.

Get it? Rise Up from the ashes - they caused their children to be burned in the fire. The Title of this chapter is Acquiescence of the Mind…

Sacrifice has long been practiced so to appease an angry god and as for the one offering the sacrifice, to "Absorb the Attributes of the Deceased".

Take note of this final thought for a moment: Since it is written that the Messiah will shine on you, isn't it also written that what is in a man is expressed on the outside? Therefore, the Messiah must first be in you and the potential of Adam is Christ. Not everyone who is reading this book has grasped the true understanding of it. Even now, concerning the influence the environment has on the man, or how detrimental not being present and mindful is to the wellbeing of the whole person. Just to make the point clear, what if instead of the promulgation of the original sin doctrine: The Frailty of Man, what if you were taught instead, the Doctrine of Infinite Potential. What if someone would have told you that Christ the original man was the first man on earth. Or better still, that Adam spoken of as the first man was not literally the first man but was a religious rendition of an ancient Near Eastern science concerning what we now know as Genetic domination, known then as the Power of the Sooth Sayer (Stay awake audience) Ancient Sooth Sayer = Modern Day Prophet. And the effects of Principles, Concepts, and Ideas in the development of man are related to the same influence that the environment has on the Atom. What if Science meaning what is truth about life was misunderstood and man therefore became superstitious for lack of knowledge during the natural process of growth and this man, we call Adam is infantile mankind and Genesis tells the story of his development and progression towards intelligence.

    Considering this point, let us turn to the writings of 2 Samuel used by so many as a prophecy of the enduring throne of Jesus. Different thought produces a new environment… Everything concerning second Samuel 7:12-14a is useful when establishing a certain doctrine but what if 14b also applied to Jesus? And why shouldn't it? By whose authority do we decide where this verse takes on new meaning or shifts its focus? Unless it is all by man's authority. This would cause a different level of thought which would provide for a more practical application relating to the children of the world who struggle with what is right and what is wrong. This scripture says, I will be a father to him, and he will be a son to me and when he does wrong, I will discipline him with a human rod and with blows from others but nevertheless, he will always be my son. The new environment: One God, One Son, Adam who did wrong, was disciplined, learned from the struggles/discipline of the world, grew from his mistakes, and proved that greater is he that is in me than he that the world sees... In his flesh, he is man but according to his spirit, Christ. Was it not the purpose of the ground since the beginning of creation to produce for the man and to feed and nourish him? Is discipline also nourishment? Did not Paul say in 1 Corinthians 15: 45-46 the first man Adam became a living being, the last Adam became a life-giving spirit. Genesis never told us who or what became of Adam. Paul knew that there is only one son of God being transformed by his journey on earth. Meaning; the Center of my being remains the same regardless of the concept I hold of myself. Man's blows are increased or lessened by the concept he holds of himself. Man's concept of himself has caused him to create conditions which would never have been known by Him, but those kingdoms which did come, revealed the kingdoms that were first in him... Acquiescence of the

Mind: His Life is full of the Kingdoms Built by Him.

Physiologic Basis for Consciousness 1. Reticular Activating System (RAS) Loose network of neurons and fibers in the brainstem which receive input from spinothalamic (sensory) pathways and project to the entire cerebral cortex. Arousal is dependent on the adequate functioning of the RAS. Arousal is purely a function of the brain stem. It does not have anything to do with the thinking parts of the brain. The fact that your patient opens his/her eyes when you call their name is an indication that their RAS (brainstem) functioning is intact, but it does not tell you if they are awake or aware.

The 1st day: Evening came and then morning: the first day. **Evening**: to intermix, intertwining of the day and night. Who will make sense of this intertwining, this intertwining of Day and Night? Conception is the result of the joining of the two essences by means of a piercing or penetration which enters or gets introduced into the being (inoculation) causes a permeation within the new being who is the same but transformed. Old passed away all has become new. Christ pierced on the cross, his hands and feet brought into subjection by piercing.

ADAM Man Convoluted but GOD

Man was once one in the Spirit of God, it was when man no longer could perceive God in himself and himself in God that he thought of himself and became an individual, no longer in union with Infinite Potential. Consciousness is the most sensitive indicator of neurological change. Consciousness can be defined as a state of general awareness of oneself and the environment. Consciousness is difficult to measure directly but it is estimated by observing how patients respond to certain stimuli. Awareness means that the brain is in harmony with the Mind. When the brain is functioning properly, one's LOC (Level of Consciousness) can be evaluated by the Pupil's response to The Fire, the Fire is the Light. When the cerebral cortex is functioning properly, the patient can interact with and interpret his environment... The Title of this chapter is Acquiescence of the Mind...

The universe has been created good and is progressing towards completion as intended by its Creator and all therein is order. Everything is in order. God is the CEO who left the continuation of bringing into being perfect order of the planet in the hands of qualified management to take up his Spirit and do as He has done, give life. Man has philosophized a religion that holds the doctrine of original sin which negates the fact of all mankind having received the Spirit of God when breath was blown into the nostrils of every living being (plant, animal, or organism, we are all organs of The Ism (interdependent parts functioning together) to create Life on Earth. **"Ism: the life force of any distinctive doctrine, cause or theory."** When one part of the body is weakened by disease and is not able to see, the rest of the healthy body compensates for it so that the entire body does not end up in the abyss. If the entire body ends up perishing, it is no question as to what was perceived of the disease which caused the whole body to partake and make home the Abyss.

Genesis 1:2 and darkness was upon the face of the deep. And the Spirit of God moved upon the face of the waters: And righteousness surfaced from that which had been made to appear as chaos and man began to understand that which caused him to destroy the earth. **Then comes** the meaning of the doctrine; **the end of the world**: Righteousness restored. The first will be last and last, first. God knows the end by the beginning, genesis is the end of darkness. Life perpetuates Life, creating within the organism sustainment for itself. Rise-up from the Ashes… The organism creates the environment for itself to thrive, that which is, is the cause of that which becomes. That which becomes is the identification of that which caused. God caused the earth to be known so that He would be known by what was created. The environment that came to be was good, for the Cause alone is

ADAM Man Convoluted but GOD

Good. Good is relative to The End of this Chapter…
Acquiescence of the Mind…

"An object at rest stays at rest and an object in motion stays in motion with the same speed and in the same direction unless acted upon by an unbalanced force."   Newton's Law of Motion

THIS CHAPTER IS DEDICATED TO VIRGINIA HAMPTON, I LOVE YOU BABY...

My mother and father were born again, regenerated by the Blood of Jesus. Their DNA had been changed by the Blood... They no longer had the Seed of Adam; they were new Seed, the Seed of Abraham through Christ. Why was their Seed born a sinner? Could Abraham and Sarah give birth to Ishmael?

Inertia and Mass: (The Woman & Rest)…

The more that an object remains in its State of Motion in relation to this chapter, (State of Mind) and the greater its mass, The Greater Man's tendency to Resist Rest.

For everyone reading this book, it is truly my desire that you have had to think about or have at least considered the ideas presented within these pages worthy of thought.

Sir William Bragg said, **"The important thing in science is not so much to obtain new facts as to discover new ways of thinking about them"**

Thus, I have attempted in closing with this chapter to present to you a new way of thinking about a particular "Fact". A "fact introduced in the 1st Book of the Bible but not fully developed until the 66th book of the same. A fact upon which I will attempt to shed light during these, the final pages of Adam Man Convoluted, but <u>GOD</u>…

God Rested, does God get tired? God fainteth not, neither is he weary: Isaiah 40:28. How does God discern time? Does the seven-day creation represent a process of evolution? For what was created on the first day could not have been created on the second and that which was created on the second could not have been created on the first. Did each day necessitate the need for the creation of something more, identifying the process required in creating and forming a thing? Did the process of creation involve time as is known to man, who himself requires time to refine raw materials from the earth. Are these the words of God describing the process of creation or ancient man's equivalent of $E=mc^2$; God being "E". Does the formation of a new heaven and a new earth require God to resume His work?

"*The God of the age -- Jehovah, Preparer of the ends of the earth, Is not wearied nor fatigued, <u>There is no searching of His understanding.</u>*"
YLT Isaiah 40:28

Within the 7 days, God prepared the end, in the end itself, a New beginning there prepared… Was the end of His work the beginning of a new dispensation? Not a dispensation of time but of the timelessness of His thought of Man?

Then I gained understanding of that which amazed me, I perceived with mine eye the city for which I waited, it descended, it was made to appear from the Heaven. Look! God's dwelling is with humanity. As I looked up into heaven, heaven did appear and I was able to see what has been made in me from the beginning, there is no limit to His understanding: The same was in the beginning was also the end... Then the One seated on the throne said, "Look! I am making everything new." I am the Alpha and the Omega, the Beginning, and the End. "It is done!" It appeared new for I could not see while I yet looked with mine eye for him on earth. In those things which mine hands have made, He was not... but that which was not made, for that is the True Self without motion, for the man who does not labor or toil is he who knows God. He who is overcoming shall inherit all things, and I will be to him -- a God, and he shall be to me -- the son. *(There is no searching of His understanding)* God Blessed the Seventh Day and, on that same day, Sanctification did also occur. Everything created, served this day in that everything created served the purpose of Man's realization of Himself. Completion revealed in the proclamation on the 6th day for He said, "It was very good". For everything was very God and His City hath no need of the sun, nor of the moon, that they may shine in it; for the glory of God did lighten it... The Glory of God is Man...

Although the light was the True Light, they were

afraid, for they imagined that the Sun would smite them by day and even the moon by night. *(There is no searching of His understanding)* Thus the story of a different Illumined Nation, not the light without but he comes from within. Remember your 40-year journey in the wilderness when your heart was revealed. He humbled you by letting you go hungry; then He gave you manna to eat, which you and your fathers had not known, so that you might learn that man does not live on bread alone. The physical light that you followed and worshipped in the desert was meant to reveal that which led you when there would be no light. God is bringing you into a good land… a New Dispensation. Abraham called it Canaan, Moses called it Sabbath, John called it heaven and Christ said that he knew the way and the way required that man should understand the physical things of Moses, for the Sabbath was made for Man, not Man for a particular Day. The seventh day is unlike all the others in that the work of completion was not wrought by thy hand, but a work Proclaimed as Sweat of the Brow. Man is Holy by the proclamation Let Us Make from that which did not first appear but became as He did proclaim. And for him to become He who was first in the beginning, God gave him bread from heaven, not earthly food but spiritual to develop the man of Spirit. Since he is Spirit, that which he is, was not made like that which could be seen, so they stumbled over Him in the desert and their harvest became food for the stomach only. Although the man was full of knowledge, yet he starved during the journey... So, God gave him manna and when they did gather, what they gathered, was enough until a New Day could be seen... and on that day, they could rest...

But what of the woman? Oh yeah, The Isah! The woman about which it is said, *"Then the Lord God made the rib He had taken from the man into a woman and brought her to the man."* Well, she is a paradox, maybe not her being but at least her name, a paradox for she who was made to appear as dead not only became alive, but he called her Eve, the Mother of all "The Living."

"You foolish Galatians! Who has hypnotized you, before whose eyes Jesus Christ was vividly portrayed as crucified?" Crucified even on a Tree...

I dedicate this to you Mama; you too were portrayed as dead so that your sons could live! If it had not been for you, I would yet be bound and this life that I now live not profound. You took beatings for your sisters and brothers bearing shame that you did not earn, I have seen your scars, whippings you took so that your children would not burn. Mother of the earth, I call you Mama! My brother's and I owe you so much, Man may never understand. This chapter is not for him though, for from him the rod has been spared. He has long been spoiled by the inheritance his sinful heart never shared. For I write as a Child of the Sand, one born of dust, beaten like sheep, they have all gone astray! I dedicate this to you Eve, counted as dead but only if they knew for whomst thou doth pray. How could you be so offensive to those to whom you spoke so true? Not just by them, even by the sons of Ham who share your hue. They hate their own skin, for the dirt and dust from which they came tell the story of you...

"Then the Lord God made the rib He had taken from the man into a woman and brought her to the man."

This one subject is so profound such that it has long been the center of debate amongst theologians and laymen alike. When discussing the forming of woman from man, questions such as if she comes from the rib of man then where is the evidence of the missing rib? How many ribs should the man or did the man have before one was taken? Does the woman have equal or fewer ribs than the man? However, the conversation should develop with the question, why not just any bone but specifically the rib bone. The next question should be what did the bones of the skeleton mean to the author of the story? Those who butchered animals for food with flint knives. Even more specifically, what did the rib cage mean to those whose ritual involved sacrificing animals as its religious duty? Required to first remove those vital organs before the ceremony could begin. What protected those organs? Greater still, what was the most valuable organ behind the ribs? Yes, the heart...

When a prophet is caused to enter a deep sleep, he is told of things his conscious mind could not understand, it is there that God speaks to the subconsciousness of the man, it is during complete rest of the conscious man that man truly has sight. It is when man is still that he may enter God's rest, he may perceive the thoughts of God. Through visions, the Mind of God may be revealed to him. Who then is the woman? The woman is the revelation of the Mind of God, and the story of Man is revealed in her. And brought her to the man: God brought revelation to the man in the likeness of the woman to see what the man would name her. What could be known about life, the woman gave to the world when she caused the whole of life to be made known by that which caused the man to die. Die that he should know Life...

The righteousness of the man began in the womb of the woman. In your mother's womb, I knew you.

Why then has the identity of the woman been hidden? For only the man to whom she chooses to give birth is she identified. Only the man to whom the woman gives life, only he is Glorified. He alone can call the woman by her name. Adam said of the woman, she is now bone of my bone and flesh of my flesh but of Eve, he proclaimed that she is the giver of life, who she is in substance is likened to the creative life force of God. From the mind of God in the form of Man who she is has been Glorified. Body from earth, substance eternal. The life source of the animal the Life Source of the Man. Eve who could only be formed while the man was in a spiritually induced sleep, the woman was the heart of the story. Eve through whom the man had to come to be called Glorified, is indeed, the Mother of All the Living.

Man known and represented superficially as Matter, even as the grey matter of the Brain lacks insulation, the outer man lacks insulation from the outer environment so that he may be made alive according to all he is able to Conceptualize. Therefore, coming to the realization; "that which is in him may not be known by what covers him." By what covers him, he has made his world known and uncovered it. Every Idea like a Star, its appearance deceiving the natural mind. What is the meaning of this grey matter of Adam's existence? Adam perceived himself as naked, when he became familiar with the environment around him, his attitude changed.

God said to Moses, no man may see Me and live with the Attitude of the World. From where comes this Attitude of Man? The attitude of the man has been taught to him; his behavior is learned. The tree represents branches of knowledge and the serpent, the irrational mind. Who then taught him to deny himself? He to whom Tuition/the Tenth was paid... Say to no man "Teacher". Tuition- the act or profession of teaching: Instruction... Intuition then is instruction which comes from within. We have understood intuition from a scientific and psychological sense implying that what is known as intuition is cumulative knowledge or knowledge formed from past experiences. (Note: pay attention to **past experiences** {*meaning having been before*} and how it is used here and then when you see it again at the end, you will understand my ending) In essence, the brain extracting subconscious thoughts from its internal vault. This not so from the spiritual perspective. The wisest man in the ancient tribe was the Shaman. This wise man was a knower, one who just knew, he just knew because he did not acquire knowledge from university, though his knowledge was universal, it was at the same time One. The power of intuition is the ability to hear from the Christ, the only begotten Son. The Shaman was known in his tribe as the healer and messenger because he spoke what he heard. What he heard was not his own words but those from the man who the world knew in appearance but perceived him not for he was the light before the Sun. John said, *"After me comes a man who has surpassed me, because He existed before me. I didn't know Him, but I came* **baptizing with water** *so*

ADAM Man Convoluted but GOD

He might be revealed to (Israel" those who **baptized/esteemed** *the physical man).*

The man experienced a perceived identity crisis so that all that existed outside of him could be made known, but who he was and to whom he related, the man found no equal until God sent the man outside of the boundaries of the physical, it was then that he could find himself. Some relate to this as strangers on earth, but I choose to express this idea as if one who is invisible, The Invisible Man. As a kid, did you ever wish that you could become invisible so that no one would see you? And if unseen by man's eye, you would then be able to do anything. Think about it, you said as a child, I would be great if I were invisible! If I were invisible, I could do anything! Now that man lives in the physical, he can do nothing Spiritually for he does not know himself. I am the invisible man for the world has made me forget myself! Man, lives on earth getting to know and establishing relationships with everyone around him but fails to establish the most important relationship. In fact, man allows himself to be defined by those with whom he does not and cannot relate. If this man was asked the question, 'Just who do you think you are?' He would do a better job defining himself from the world's perspective, The World's Standard of man. As for knowing himself, Adam the "Lord" in the Garden, **made** Invisible, **became** divisible for the world proved that he was capable of being disunited from the total sum of Himself, the product of the Serpent who defined him. Yes, you are invisible, not to the world but the world hid him from himself for those are they who crucified him and rendered him useless by attaching the label; you sin for you are just a man!

Yes, Just a Man, so therefore you must be fragile, fragile to the point of nonexistent in comparison to the Indivisible. What does this mean, this invisible man? What has this to do with the end? By the sweat of your brow shall you eat your food. Man has been toiling under the sun to eat his food. What food? Where would you be had you not eaten? What would be his occupation had he not sewed together his own clothes? How could he be that which he was not? How could that which he was not, be who he was in the beginning unless that which he knew as the beginning had already been the world that became void and formless destroyed by those to whom perceived work as wisdom, and Rest as Death? The World which he would come to know by his works was void and formless for man's works destroyed the world! Then God moved Upon the Waters… The End!

And then comes this, Mystery; {the Sabbath is God's Message} to HIS Intelligent Man. Adam does not toil! Adam stop toiling and Be! God knows you already are!

ADAM Man Convoluted but GOD

You are Convoluted because of What you put your hands to and not your Mind! He took your Mind captive when he gave you food! (Those physical things) He traded the Spiritual Man for the thing which never existed: The World given was full of Life, He was the Life of the World... The man became Empty and Void!
ADAM, Man Convoluted! but GOD...

ADAM Man Convoluted but GOD

About The Author...
as told by The Minister

Born April 21, 1971, in the Divine Savior Hospital of York S.C. to Thomas L. Hampton and Virginia Mintz Hampton. He is the only son from Thomas and the second son of three from Virginia. His father Thomas was a Minister and founder of "The Chosen Few Ministry" in Charlotte N.C. Virginia was the daughter of Rosa Bell Mintz and Rev. Lee W. Mintz founder of St. James church of God in Orangeburg S.C.

When I became a man, I put away the childish things and became fully-grown. (I learned the difference between Concrete and Abstract; Literal and Figurative) I knew right from wrong, real from the imagined. When I became a man, I lost my dream! I lost the power to "Make Believe"!

Today, he views himself as in relation to religious indoctrination "A Free Thinker", one who does not easily conform to religious suggestion and dogma as Divine Word and this not an acquired eccentricity received from life's experiences but an inheritance. As a toddler, he would wander away from his home to experience his quiet rural neighborhood or to visit with friends of the family, in particular, his godmother a few houses away to dine with them; as he has always possessed a palate for fine, flavorful cuisine. By the age of four, he and his best friend at the time, attempted to prepare a flavorful dish that did not turn out so well for such young chefs or the Easter chicken. One Easter, when his parents asked him what he wanted for Easter, the author requested a biddy, (a baby chicken) and his parents got one for him; a soft cuddly yellow biddy.

    One thing that the minister has learned about the author is that he is very analytical and perceptive. Even from childhood, he would watch carefully while Virginia would be in the kitchen cooking, taking note of skills passed on to his mother from her mother Rosa who was the best undisputed cook of the family. With his brief training by the age of four, he put what he observed from his mother into action, he, and his toddler friend, decided to pluck the feathers from his live biddy and put it in the oven to have bake chicken as a main course. Hearing the frantic chirps of a distressed baby chicken, Virginia ran to the bird's rescue and pulled it still alive from that hot inferno. That biddy grew up into one of the fiercest roosters this minister has ever seen!

Not only is he a free thinker, even at an early age, he wanted people to be treated respectfully and morally. One day when he was around the age of three or four, he, his mother and oldest brother went to a softball game, and Virginia caught a homerun ball hit across the fence but was unable to keep it because the author cried and emphatically cried because he said that his mother was going to get in trouble for stealing the softball. Growing up, it was easily seen by those who could carefully observe him, that he would follow in his father's path and become a minister. Second thought, it may not have easily been seen by some who knew him very well outside of his parent's watchful eye. His close friends probably never imagined that a boy with a hot temper such as his would ever follow his father's path and seek the peace of "Higher Spiritual Understanding". This though was not by happenstance; this desire was acquired through prayer and training by a father and mother who knew that the path was narrow, but their son enjoyed the broad. On Saturdays, Thomas would teach the author about principles of the Bible and have Bible study with his only son. One day, Thomas said to the author, "on this Saturday coming, I'm going to teach you son how to fast, we are going to fast until 12o'clock noon". Well, said the acutely sharp thinker to himself; "I'll just get up at about 11 a.m. and fast for about an hour with daddy, that shouldn't be too bad, I will only have to suffer for an hour without food".

When Saturday dawned, Thomas being the acutely

sharp and perceptive thinker he was said; "I know my son is going to attempt to sleep in so let me help him get the full benefit of this training that will strengthen his spiritual man and teach him to starve the physical man who desires to be like and crave the things of the world". Bright and early Saturday, the author heard the familiar voice of his father saying; "Son, its 0530, we are fasting today for six hours, get up and be ready by 0600"! Thomas had a highly effective method of teaching scripture to his son. He would give the author a passage of scripture and let him study the passage for a while and then ask him to explain in his own words what the scripture revealed. Never would Thomas tell the author if his explanation was right or wrong but would only nod and say, "I see." On one Sunday in the late 70's or early 80's, Thomas took his son, the author to an Atrium in Charlotte N.C. to listen to Shirley Caesar preach. After her sermon, Thomas asked the author; "Tell me what you got from the sermon in your own words, and do you agree with the message?"

Her sermon that day focused on the authority and power that Satan exhibits toward man and how man should not take the enemy lightly. The author explained to his father his opinion and exegesis of the sermon in these words; "She gave the Devil too much power!" Again, Thomas only nodded his head and said, "I see". These early years were only the dawning of the light that would begin to illuminate and permeate the life and experience of the author who brings these words to you. Thanks for your interest and purchase of this book, the author prays that the light will dawn on you and cause you to express it like only my Dad could; "I see"! Now that I am a man of age and understanding, I now See why my father only nodded at my analysis and assumptions. He understood that I could only walk in the path of my own understanding. My imagination was the seed of my reality; what I was able to see was my Own World, of which, **I Am** Master… To see through my father's eyes would cause me to stumble. He was teaching me How to think and not merely what to think! I now know how to *"Make Believe"*. Which is The Gift from God, a Wheel in a Wheel…

My dream has come true, thank you! What you believe in your heart does not exist until you <u>Make your Belief</u> *in the beginning was the Word and the Word was with God, but life did not exist because the Word was in God, only God knew that Life was in the Word.* When the Word became flesh, then was God **known!**

May you look with your eyes and apprehend with your mind.

May you capitulate yourself to God so that the world

will not blind you to see but not perceive

the Unseen! The Minister

ADAM Man Convoluted but GOD

...That's why the pupil of one eye can change when you **Shine The Light Into Your Other Eye.**

BIBLIOGRAPHY

-Gebler, Karl Von, *Galileo Galilei And the Roman Curia.* C. Kegan Paul Co., I, Paternoster Square, London.: 1879.

-Armstrong, A.H, *The Cambridge History of Later Greek, and Early Medieval Philosophy.* Cambridge at the University Press, 1967

-Vincent, Marvin R, Vincent's *Word Studies of the New Testament* Peabody, MA: Hendrickson Publishers (1886)

-Köstenberger, Andreas J. *Invitation to Biblical Interpretation: Exploring the Hermeneutical Triad of History, Literature, and Theology.* Invitation to Theological Studies Series. Grand Rapids, MI: Kregel Publications, 2011.

-Dawson, Christopher. *Religion and the Rise of Western Culture.* image books ed. New York: Doubleday, 1991.

-Neville. *The Power of Awareness.* New York: Jeremy P. Tarcher/Penguin, 2012.

-Howard, David M. *An Introduction to the Old Testament Historical Books.* Chicago: Moody Publishers, 2007.

-http://infed.org/mobi/john-dewey-my-pedagogical-creed/.

-Delitzsch, Franz. *Biblical Commentary On the Book of Job.* Vol. 1, *(Classic Reprint).* Norwood, Mass.: Forgotten Books, 2012.

-Baring, Anne, and Jules Cashford. *The Myth of the Goddess: Evolution of an Image.* New York, N.Y.: Penguin, 1993.

-Kittd, Gerhard. *Theological Dictionary of the New Testament (Volume III).* Grand Rapids, MI: William B. Eerdmans

Publishing Company, 1964.

-Merriam-Webster. *The Merriam-Webster dictionary.* Home ed. Springfield, Mass.: Merriam Webster, 1998.

-Longman, Tremper, and III & Raymond B. Dillard. *An Introduction to the Old Testament.* 2nd ed. Grand Rapids, Mich.: Zondervan, 2006.

-Benner, Jeff A. *The Ancient Hebrew Lexicon of the Bible: Hebrew Letters, Words and Roots Defined Within Their Ancient Cultural Context.* College Station, TX: Virtualbookworm.com Publishing, 2005.

-Scherman, with a commentary anthologized from the rabbinic writings by Nosson. *The Chumash: The Torah, Haftaros and Five Megillos = Ḥamishah Ḥumshe Torah.* 11th ed. Brooklyn, N.Y.: Mesorah Pubns Ltd, 2000.

-Hensley, Adam. Source: Logia, 27 no 3 Holy Trinity 2018, p 41-44. Publication Type: Article, Database: <u>ATLA Religion Database with ATLASerials</u>

-Merrill, Eugene H. Source: Criswell Theological Review, 14 no 1 **Fall** 2016, p 15-22. Publication Type: Article, Database: <u>ATLA Religion Database with ATLASerials</u>

-Zondervan. *NIV Archaeological Study Bible: An Illustrated Walk Through Biblical History and Culture.* not ed. Grand Rapids: Zondervan, 2006.

-Strong, James. *The New Strong's Exhaustive Concordance of the Bible: With Main Concordance, Appendix to the Main Concordance, Topical Index to the Bible, Dictionary of the Hebrew Bible, Dictionary of the Greek Testament.* Nashville, Tenn.: Thomas Nelson Inc, 1990.

-Mortenson, Dr Terry. *Searching for Adam: Genesis and the Truth About Man's Origin.* Master Books, 2016.

-Wright, Ross. *Holman Christian Standard Apologetics Study Bible Brown Bonded Leather.* Place of publication not identified: Holman Bible Pub, 2007.

-Bellah, Robert N. *Religion in human evolution : from the Paleolithic to the Axial Age.* Cambridge, Mass: Belknap Press of Harvard University Press, 2011.

-*ivp Bible Dictionary Series.* Vol. 1], *Dictionary of the Old Testament: Pentateuch.* Downers Grove, Ill.: InterVarsity Press, ©2003.

-*The Hebrew Bible Today: An Introduction to Critical Issues.* Louisville, Ky.: Westminster John Knox Press, ©1998.

-*The Anchor Bible Dictionary.* New York: Doubleday, ©1992.

Bright, John. *A History of Israel.* 2nd ed. Philadelphia: Westminster Press, 1972.

ADAM Man Convoluted, but GOD…

Let those who have been made Filthy, continuing being Filthy, but Adam was made In God's Image and God's Image is Christ…
AMEN

Read Only If You Wish to Go Beyond...

When God took the man and placed him in the Garden, told him to make a choice between life and death, what would the outcome have been if the man would not have eaten from either of the trees? Was the man dead or alive? Was he in transition? Was he where we are today? Are we that man named Adam, not having life nor death but alive? If alive what kind of being are we, those who can talk to God? We know God, does God know death? Man was never dead; he was with Him in the beginning. Adam heard the voice of God in his mind and went looking for the voice he had heard. Don't you hear God talking to you, where is God when you hear Him? Where is He talking to you from?

> *Psalm 8:3-5; "When I observe Your heavens, the work of Your fingers, the moon and the stars, which You set in place, what is man that You remember him, the son of man that You look after him? You made him little less than God and crowned him with glory and honor...*

Other versions or translations of this same scripture use the statement, little less than angels, rather than little less than God. The word is Elohim, let's look at verse 5 in the

ADAM Man Convoluted but GOD

Orthodox Jewish Version: For Thou hast made him a little lower than elohim [or Elohim, Gn 1:27 Bereshis 1:27 OJB So G-d created humankind in His own tzelem, in the tzelem Elohim (image of G-d) created He him; and hast crowned him with kavod and hadar. And crowned him with Kavod (Honor) and Hadar (Glory). Man was created with Hardar and Kavod in the beginning but the translator of scripture, rather than describing Glorified Adam, described himself according to the state he or they believed themselves to be when the seventy interpreted The Writings.

Who God crowns as King, cannot be dethroned except in his own mind, can he become less than The Tzelem Elohim… But what did he eat which caused him to see himself as less than?

Adam and Eve ate from a Tree… Today we have heard the fallen message preached by man who also coils on a lifted platform to deliver false messages. Messages concerning the Dust which he does not understand. Genesis 1:6 - Then God said, "Let Us **make** man in Our image, according to Our likeness… The Spiritual Adam. Genesis 2:7 - Then the Lord God **formed** the man out of the dust from the ground and breathed the breath of life into his nostrils, and the man became a living being… The Physical Form. Do you see that? The difference between the spiritual and the physical? The word Make comes from the Hebrew word Asah which is defined by three words, accomplish, advance, and appoint.

To be interpreted loosely, Make, in its broadest sense could mean if using the word advance, could mean "Let Us Become Man" or Let the elohim take a physical form and become Man. Man is the Physical form of the Spiritual… What about the Tree, that elevated platform from where the serpent delivered its message? Let me explain…

The tree represents the connection between the spiritual realm and the material world. Every tree was once a seed, if not a physical seed, it became what it is today from a thought seed. The seed possesses infinite potential within itself, it is what it can become. The seed is the principle of life. The seed is complex. Adam, the one formed from the ground, could digest physical food, so he ate. The Spiritual Man does not live on physical bread at all but lives through the physical. You are what you eat, what you eat influences the physical body only, the Spiritual Man has been Crowned and is not affected by what the Man digests. The physical man only 'believes', the Spiritual Man 'Knows' and because of this difference, the physical man believes that he has become less than Glorified and, in his mind, he falls because of what he has eaten. What you take in, your subconscious mind believes, and a person becomes the total sum of what is believed as true! Man believes that he is ONLY DUST!

Man from dust: dust comes from transition. Earth unsettled causes dust to rise. A Force like spirit could cause dust to rise. Dust could be translated as not yet finished. Dust could also be an unfinished thought. Earth as a concrete thing, dust as abstract. Dust could also mean foundation. When God was laying the foundation of the earth, He created man for there could be no earth without man to rule it. I'm thinking about the dust of the earth, this is not the dust of the earth that is mentioned in Genesis 2.

Theory

1) Dust- Hebrew Chumash: Man is not formed from dust, but man is "the Man of dust" Hashem God formed "the man of dust" from the ground

   a. since God gave form to the man of dust, as dust, the man had no form.

    b. this dust of which man consisted, was from the **Ground**...What is the ground and how is it different from land?

2) Rain gave life to the earth for without rain, nothing sprouted. The same is mentioned for man, also without him nothing sprouted although, in the ground everything that could sprout existed.

3) Dust: dry particles of matter so light that it may be raised and carried by the wind. Dust then being or having relation to spirit which moves by the breath/wind (ruach) of God.
    a) Man of dust therefore is the man of spirit
    b) Man is spirit from heaven, man is formed from the ground.

4) Ground: foundation/principle of life. Who man is to be, he has been from the foundation of the earth. (This understanding is not literal; this can't be understood from physical matter) Matter must first be alive/formed in thought.

God mentions the earth and the land: the dust of the earth to the concrete thinker living in the desert, is as a man walking and sees dust under his feet becoming a cloud of dust lifted into the air causing limited vision: dust of the earth is as the stars of the sky. The stars of the sky appear as particles of dust floating in the air. Man is made from the same stuff: particulate matter that comes from the heavens. Man is an aggregate of heavenly and earthly matter. God formed the man out of the dust of the ground, not the land. God formed the man out of the ground: foundation/principle of life that is in all the earth, the same life of God. Man is the foundation of life here on earth! God is life! Man is the Life who comes from heaven to live on Earth! Man is God from Heaven who settles on earth and populates/replenishes the land with Himself in Man. Christ is God in transition, Man lives on land as God does in heaven, everything exists because of God, everything that exists below heaven exists because Man has willed the Earth.

Paul recognized that Man was in God in the beginning... Well maybe not Paul but the Ephesians caused Paul to understand Verse 1:4 "according as He did choose us in him before the foundation of the world, for our being holy and unblemished before Him, in love." Youngs literal translation. For those who can only perceive man as lowly dust are mistaken. The dust of man is the power of God to give life to matter and this matter is the dust of the ground. The dust of the ground is the life power of the word. Simply put, man understands the dust to be low only after it has been trodden upon but the dust in the beginning was from the mind of God for nothing existed and everything was good, everything was God. Are we to understand then that God made those Holy things from his mind lowly? Dust itself did not exist until the work of a perfect creation had begun and in the sense of saw dust: formed while the master carpenter creates/fashions and turns raw wood into a "mansion" house of God. Man gave this negative connotation to dust for dust is the thought of God; man, the handy work of God.

There is only one reality and God by Nature created that reality. Man has never been dead for man has always existed in that reality; man is God's reality. When he awakes, he will see his dream, he will realize that his life was ordered by himself.

The Word

Paul told the Romans to do exactly what God told You and Me in the Garden: God blessed them (with His Holy Ghost (Ruach) and said to Us, "Replenish the Earth and Subdue it.") God has commanded the Earth to produce for His Son. When the Son speaks, the Earth hears God when the Son resembles the Father and speaks from where the

Father is… God said whatever you put your hands to, will prosper.

THERE. IS. BUT. ONE. MIND, the Mind of God. In the Garden, God gave them His Mind and told them to Make the Earth His Footstool… The word Subdue means Footstool in Hebrew. Where else have you come across the word Footstool in the Bible? One place is Psalm 99:5; Exalt the Lord our God; bow in worship at His footstool. I remember going to church bowing at the altar to worship God. That was not true worship, that was a representation of what worship is. Bowing in worship at His Footstool is to bring all that is on the Earth into subjection to The Mind of God. How did the hovering Spirit of God bring order to Chaos, He did it by giving The Son of Man His Ruach… Guess where the Altar of God is where we should bow before Him? The Earth… Is His Footstool, The Earth is the heap of dirt, the Earth is the Altar where Man should humble himself and worship God… I saw the Angels day and night around the throne worshiping God. (Revelation 4:8): Each one of those angels represent each one of us… On Earth as it is in Heaven!

After Christ resisted, the Angels came and served

Him. Jesus was facing the same thoughts or situation as Adam and Eve and you and me. He was at a point, a crossroad that we face. This was the Cross, this was the point of his journey where He revealed the Nature of the Son of God. For me, He became Christ, the resurrected Adam, the message for all mankind, He resisted even unto death. In Matthew 4, during the temptation, Jesus was tested on 3 areas, the same three areas that Adam and Eve failed: (1. Food; he challenged Him to turn that which is not edible into food. (God told Adam not to eat: consume, preoccupy himself with the fruit of that tree. Listen to this… In essence, God told Adam that he must not "EAT from it", allow that tree to be a source of strength, nourishment, or sustenance (Give authority to that which is unfruitful). In other words, Adam had no business giving life to the fruit of death. There was no fruit on the tree, but the fruit of disobedience is death. Man added fruit to the tree by "EATing from it!" The quote unquote Devil wanted Christ to add fruit to that same tree by turning stone into bread. We are having debates today concerning what type of fruit was on the tree, search Genesis and see who mentioned fruit on the Tree of the Knowledge of Good and Evil. Again, there was No fruit on that tree, except for the authority and freedom of choice that the man has which he gave to the tree to produce a life outside of God's Garden also known as Death. Death is the absence of Life. Evil means the absence of Righteousness. Evil is not an entity, Evil does not have a body or form, Man Gives FORM to Evil…

'Follow me, I'm getting deeper'.

I don't like the taste of fish from lakes, ponds, and streams. To me, the fish taste like dirt. But I love going deep sea fishing. Some people would not dare go out into the deep dark ocean in a boat for hours to catch fish. They fear the unknown, they rather fish from the shore and catch little fish but the meat comes from Deep in the unknown waters. I would like to thank all of you who have purchased this book and getting into my Yacht with me so that we can go deeper.

I Love Deep Sea Fishing

I have been studying the book of Zechariah, the contemporary of Haggai and I noticed something, God gave me a revelation… Both Zechariah and Haggai ministered to the same people, but from "Different Perspectives". Haggai reproved the people for their failure to rebuild the temple, while Zechariah encouraged the people by presenting to them the Coming Glory of the Lord. They were saying the same thing with different approaches. Haggai was preaching "in a sense" condemnation to motivate the people to rebuild the Temple but Zechariah on the other hand was preaching Spiritual Transformation, the rebuilding of the Human Temple so that the Messiah could come, the Glory could come, so that God could Inhabit Man on earth "Emmanuel". Not a building made by hand…

Before the people could have a Heavenly experience, the earthly temple had to be destroyed and rebuilt. In other words, Evil has to be destroyed. How do you destroy Evil? By the transformation of your Mind. How is this you ask. I'm glad you asked… I know some of you are saying that the Greatest lie or trick of the Devil is to cause people to believe that he doesn't exist. Are you still in the boat? He does exist, but only in the Fallen World of reality created by disobedient Adam. And since sin entered the world through Adam, only can sin be destroyed by Adam because Adam is its Author. (You create your own reality) Evil only exists where righteousness does not. Where there is the lack of Truth, Evil resides. When Light enters the room, Darkness dissipates. Darkness only appears when there is no light… Ignorance of the Truth gives Life to darkness. Now think about redemption: WE'RE DEEP-SEA FISHING NOW! Stay on the Boat with me.

Make your own attitude that of Christ Jesus, who, existing in the form of God, did not consider equality with God as something to be used for His own advantage. Instead, He EMPTIED Himself by assuming the form of a slave, taking on the likeness of men. And when He had come as a man in His external form, He humbled Himself by becoming obedient to the point of death — even to death on a cross. (Philippians 2:5-8)

Taking on the likeness of men. **The likeness of men…**

They asked me did Christ imagine the conversation he had with the so-called Devil? No, but he entered Adam's reality, He Emptied Himself and had a conversation with a creature of Man's imagination, which has become the reality of man so that He could rescue and resurrect Adam. To come to this world, Christ had to lower himself down to man's reality and consider as real what has plagued man for so long and to destroy the fallen image so that Adam could once again see the Image of God in Himself.

This is the Coming of the Glory of God that Zechariah was preaching. But man likes to stand on the edge of the waters and fish. Tell them to come get in My Yacht and let's Travel Beyond...

www.ingramcontent.com/pod-product-compliance
Lightning Source LLC
Chambersburg PA
CBHW071740150426
43191CB00010B/1640